CERTIFICATE
for
FREE TICKETS

Michael Neeley, founder and CEO of Your Authority Blueprint, cordially invites you and a friend to attend one of our live events as our guest. Please go to www.YourAuthorityBlueprint.com/Gift to register today.

If you do not have access to a computer, you may contact us at 831-236-6868 to register over the phone.

This offer is available to all purchasers of "The Art of Forgetting" by Michael Neeley. This offer is limited to the Your Authority Blueprint Live event only, and registration to the event is subject to availability of space and/or changes to the schedule or program. This is a limited time offer, and may or may not extend to events beyond the date shown above. The value of this free ticket for two people is $1,994 at the time of printing, and is subject t change. Participants are responsible for travel to and from the event, and for meals while on location. A refundable seat deposit will be required upon registration in order to secure your seat. This deposit will be refunded only upon your arrival at the event on the first day. This is in order to prevent "no-shows" and to be able to provide the venue with an accurate attendee count.

The Art of
FORGETTING

Your First Step Toward Lasting Change

Michael Neeley

AUTHORSOURCE

For my beloved wife, Meghan ...

who continually reminds me to forget.

Contents

Introduction

First off, I want to thank you for taking the time to not only purchase my book, but to actually start reading it. The last thing on earth I would want is to create another shelf-help book.

Yeah ... that's not a typo. You know that genre—the books you buy with the greatest intentions and then they sit there adorning your bookcase for years ... untouched.

So, thanks. You've picked it up, and you're actually reading it.

I also want you to be forewarned.

I've been complimented on my writing style by many people, and the common thread seems to be the sentiment, "Michael, you write like you talk," to which I reply, "You mean slow and with a southern drawl?"

"No, but it always feels like you're just sitting there talking to me."

Aha. Got it.

Well ... I have to be honest here, as I was reading the final draft before going to print, even I had to re-read a few sentences just to get what the heck I was saying. So I apologize in advance if my way of speak-writing throws you off track from time to time.

This book has been a cross between a labor of love and the child that lived under the stairs—sometimes embraced and snuggled, and others completely neglected. If you are a writer yourself, you likely know what I'm talking about.

And if you've got a big message yourself, something that's been nagging at you to get it out to the world, I hope you'll visit my website (www.YourAuthorityBlueprint. com) and even take advantage of the free tickets offered with this book.

One of my areas of expertise is helping visionary solopreneurs (coaches, authors, speakers, consultants, and holistic practitioners) go from being the best-kept secret to the "Go-To" Expert in their field. I'd be happy to support you, as well.

In the meantime, I hope you enjoy my book!

Chapter One

How It All Got Started

Damn! I did it again.

DAMN!! I did it again!

DAMN!!! I DID IT, YET AGAIN!!!

What? What did I do?

Have you ever had this happen? You've found yourself *senselessly* repeating the same mistake?

There is an idiom I'm sure you've heard: Fool me once, shame on you; fool me twice, shame on me. I'd like to make a couple of small adjustments for self-application of this statement: Fool me once, shame on *me*; fool me twice, shame on *me*; Fool me a third time, WTF?!?

Good things come in threes. Bad things come in threes. Celebrity deaths come in threes. Third time is a charm. Yada yada yada.

Maybe you are among the few living beings to which my little adage does not apply. But in the event that you are not, I'm willing to bet the price of this book that what you are about to discover was the culprit behind your trifecta.

It's your memory!

What a double-edged sword! Memory serves *and* corrupts. It is still an absolute necessity, even once you've discovered it acts as a double agent at times.

You might be wondering, *What on earth is this guy talking about?! Is he insane?!* Well, the jury is still out on that one, but if you'll hear me out, you can cast your vote later.

Like you, in my everyday life, I frequently perform many tasks automatically. It often starts with a shower (or earlier, if the automated part of my day gets engaged in the way I stretch before getting out of bed).

Muscle memory kicks in while my mind turns over the reins to my body. Letting the body take control, my conscious mind is left to relax, wander, hypostulate, create, and more.

Sometimes, so complete is the subjugation of the mind, that I would be hard-pressed to recount, in any detail, my physical actions. This is called going on "auto-pilot," and I've been known to do it while driving. Scary, I know.

One day, this became so extensive that it manifested itself in the performance of my job. Okay. I should have written that all in CAPS, but I didn't want you to think that I was shouting at you.

Let me say it again. "This became so extensive that it manifested itself in the performance of my job." Hmmmmm, maybe CAPS is the only way to really get across the significance of this, but I'll try another way.

Imagine that you've done a particular task, or interacted with someone, in such a repetitive fashion that you have developed the ability to perform that task while letting your mind depart your body. Not that it will physically drop out of your head and roll away (at least, I hope not), but your mind isn't consciously involved with what your body is doing.

Now, if you are, let's say, filling out a report or filing paperwork, that's not really a big issue.

That, however, was not what I was doing.

I was interacting with another individual. A doctor, no less. I was a pharmaceutical sales rep, and I was having a discussion with this doctor about the benefits of my particular drug. AND I WAS ON AUTO-PILOT!

Sorry. I didn't mean to yell.

Later, as I was sitting in my company car and making some notes about our interaction, I could not recall a single word of our conversation. Strangely, that was not the part that startled me or sparked my idea for this book.

This next part did...

I *knew exactly what to write in my notes because every conversation I'd had with this doctor in the past had been virtually the same.*

I knew, before we even spoke, what he was going to

say. He'd said it hundreds of times before, and I was sure he would say it hundreds of times in the future.

In that moment, I realized that our fate (as a relationship) was sealed. I had set up, at least in my mind, both a parameter and a perimeter in which my experience with him would reside.

That made me realize I had a BIG problem. And this book was generated out of my search for a solution.

Chapter Two

What This Book Is About

From the time we could move about as an infant on the floor, slowly, but surely, we began to draw correlations between cause and effect. As time went on, we seared these imprints into our minds.

Of our own volition, we came to the conclusion that certain pieces of furniture were easier to hold onto than others; that when we batted our little hands at the mobile over our crib, things would start moving.

As we moved into our toddler years, these correlations were reinforced and added to by our parents. "Don't touch the stove; you'll burn your fingers." "Don't get soap in your eyes or it will sting." "Don't run with scissors, or ..." Well, you get the point.

At that age, we challenged the truth to many of these tenets. But as our adolescent years approached, most of these ideas became cemented as fact.

I'm not knocking them by any means. Heck, without most of what we remembered throughout those years, many of us wouldn't be here today (or, at least, not here with all of our appendages). These lessons in life served a great purpose, and still do today.

The problem began when we started to use that same formula for *things that do change*. Like people, ideas, even our pets, to name a few. Why shouldn't we use the formula? It's easy. Seems to be pretty darn accurate. I've already grown accustomed to its application. Makes sense, doesn't it?

And so we did. And we do. We apply this same formula every day, in many, many ways. Do you always drive the same route to work? Always brush your teeth a certain way? Always answer the phone in the same tone, or with the same phrase? Now there may be a few of you to which none of these apply. But stick around; I'm willing to bet that you'll recognize a few habits of your own.

Did I say, "habits"? Well, yeah. At least, that's what

they are now. But they didn't start out that way. Most of our current habits started out as a choice. We drove a certain route home, concluded that it was the fastest, most economic, most scenic (whatever floated your boat at the time), and decided to always use that route.

You discovered the most effective way to brush your teeth in the least amount of time (and by golly, you're sticking to it). Do that thirty days in a row and, voila! Another habit is born.

I'm not saying that these are bad things. I'm just asking that you look at them. Most of your habits are done subconsciously. Have you ever been driving somewhere familiar to you, and the next thing you know, you've lost ten minutes of your trip because you went into auto-pilot while your mind wandered elsewhere? I've done it enough times to scare myself.

Sometimes we tune out so completely, it's almost like a meditation. I've gotten ready for work with my mind so intent on the day's schedule that I couldn't tell you if I washed my hair or not (but I'd be willing to bet I did, since it is so ingrained into my routine).

Even with that degree of habit, you're still not in major danger of living a less than desirable life.

But try this: Go to work for ten days straight (okay, maybe just five) and have your bad-mood boss yell at you for something trivial. You've now imprinted an image of your boss as an ill-tempered tyrant on your mind (if he wasn't that beforehand).

Yes, with negative impressions, the imprint takes hold much more rapidly than positive ones. The next thing you know, you get up for work ALREADY EXPECTING TO GET YELLED AT FOR SOMETHING. (Sorry, I didn't mean to raise my voice so loud.)

Here's another one, maybe a little closer to home: Every time you talk to your spouse about taking a European vacation, he or she goes into a huge rant about all of the bills and how impossible it would be to afford the trip. After about five to ten attempts, you give up and *assign your spouse a label.*

The label could be many different things. You could decide that he or she just doesn't value the same things as you. All they care about is money. Or maybe they're selfish and only care about what *they* want.

Whatever you decide, it's going to stick. And the next time you think of asking to make a major household purchase, you'll already be anticipating a problem.

When I worked in the pharmaceutical industry as a sales rep, this occurred on a much simpler level. I knew which doctors would give me time and which ones would simply sign for samples and walk away. I knew which docs would enjoy a personal conversation and which ones were strictly business. In short, I knew which ones were the "nice guys" and which ones were the jerks.

The problem is, once you (and I) have pigeonholed someone, including your spouse, your parents, and your children, you've *limited their ability to be anything different.*

"Wait a minute," you say. "How can 'I' make anyone be any specific way?"

It's not so much that they are going to be that way with everyone all the time. But, in your world, you've limited their space to fit your perception of them.

If you expect someone to act a certain way, you'll have a tendency to interpret any action they take to fit into your idea of them. On top of that, they are receiving a subliminal (or subconscious) request from you to show up in your world that way!

I once had a manager that seemed extremely punitive to me. No matter what I did, he always seemed to find something wrong, and was sure to bring it to my attention. My interpretation of him kept him in that space, AND IT KEPT ME IN THE SPACE OF SEEING HIM THAT WAY. (There I go yelling again.)

Finally, after a couple of unbearable months, I had to bring it to his attention. I told him I was ready to quit and had been interviewing with other companies.

It was a big surprise to me when he explained that he was only acting that way because he had really high hopes for me within the company, and that he didn't see any value in telling me the things I was already doing well. The room for improvement was only in my shortcomings.

Let me repeat that again.

The room for improvement was only in my shortcomings.

After we'd cleared the air, I understood him much better and our relationship improved dramatically. He also learned that I was the kind of employee who needed a dose of positive feedback to help swallow the criticism.

By the way, I was not the only representative who was having a problem with his management style. Other managers came to the rescue and gave him some coaching on handling his hires. As he was new to the position, he took the training well and made some major adjustments.

This allowed all of us to see him in a whole new way. It took some time, but it was time well spent.

How does this apply to your job? Do you call on the same clients over and over? Are you a manager that supervises a large staff? I can hardly think of a job that doesn't require some interaction with a variety of people and personality types.

For those of you who do work with the same folks on a regular basis, I'd bet you can already tell me how they would respond to most of your inquiries.

I know I could tell you which of my doctors would go out for a dinner program and which ones wouldn't.

Oh, and there's a little devil here. It's called pride. Most of us are even *proud* of the fact that we can tell in advance what someone is going to think or say. Come on … aren't you?

How many of you could tell me, with hardly a doubt in your mind, what your spouse/significant other would say if you went home right now and said you wrecked the car? Or that you just lost your job?

Like it or not, we have stored images of interactions with others that influence our behavior—and theirs.

How does this work? How do *we* influence *their* behavior?

Check out these two different forms of the same question: 1) "Could I borrow your car?" 2) "You wouldn't want to lend me your car, would you?" The second example may be a bit to the extreme (although most of you have probably heard someone ask a similarly styled question before), but I want you to understand this: Even if you word the question as in example #1, if you are thinking in terms of example #2, what do you think that person's going to hear? They're going to hear that *you don't really expect them to say yes*, and probably for good cause. If you wouldn't lend yourself the car, why should they?

Of course, if the car's owner we're speaking of always lets you borrow the car, you're going to go into the situation with a clear expectation of getting the car. Heck, you might even just say, "Hey, where're the car keys?" And you'd probably be downright surprised if you got a "no."

On the other hand, if the owner had just bought the car, and it's his pride and joy, you would already be feeling pretty positive about a negative response. Even if you ask in simple terms—such as "Hey, can I borrow your car?"—you know he's going to say, "No."

You can further emphasize your commitment to a "no" by adding a bit of begging: "Hey, if you'll loan me your car, I'll bring it back full of gas, all polished and waxed. Could I, please?"

So that's how you influence the behavior of others. Research has shown that the greatest percentage of communication between people is non-verbal. Body language and tonality make up the greater part of our communication. No matter how hard you try to mask your preconceived notions about an interaction, your subconscious "self" is going to give you away.

And that communication speaks far louder than words.

Well, damn, if that's the problem and it's so ingrained in us, what do we do?

You forget.

Now I'm not saying you erase all of your memories like the film, *Eternal Sunshine of the Spotless Mind*. Instead, you need to do what I call "Selective Forgetfulness."

You're going to remember the things that serve you and forget those that don't. We've learned them from childhood through college and beyond, and the ones you want to remember don't usually need the noted consequences attached (i.e., Don't put your hand in the fire, or you'll get burned).

Nor do you want to forget any of the list I've provided below (you may add to it):

- Look both ways before you cross the street.

- Do not take a bath in scalding water.

- Make sure your boss is out of hearing distance before calling him names.

- Make sure the police officer's back is turned before you flip him off.

- Never shout, "Theatre!" in a crowded firehouse.

- Never look a gift horse in the mouth.

Now I'm not sure about that last one. Is it because it might bite you? Of course, if the Spartans had looked the Trojan Horse in the mouth, they might have lived a bit longer. On second thought, let's just drop that last one.

Here are some things it might be helpful to forget: just about everything else!

At least everything that relates to people.

PEOPLE CHANGE!

They do if we let them. The greatest gift you can give someone is the opportunity to surprise you. Look at each interaction fresh, with no expectations, and allow yourself to be surprised.

PEOPLE CHANGE!

Let them! See them always with new eyes and give up any of your preconceived notions about them.

By the way, many times our preconceived notions were given to us by someone else *even before we've met the person.*

An old Buddhist tenet says that you learn nothing about the person someone speaks of, but much about the person doing the speaking. Actually, I think I just made that up by paraphrasing a comment from a Buddhist author.

So there's a practical example: In my last sentence, you learned nothing about Buddhism, but a great deal about me: I like to make things up. Even if that is not necessarily true of me, it would be of great benefit for you to forget it.

You see the game we play in our minds? We actually strive to store all of this information that allows us to pigeonhole someone, just so we can predict their actions or reactions.

Why?

Because predictability is safe! Ask any trial attorney. They are trained to never ask a question they don't already know the answer to. Too much risk otherwise. Unsafe. And not many of us like unsafe territory.

The problem? Where does possibility for change, possibility for learning, possibility for growth exist? Only in the unknown, ergo unsafe, zone.

Scary stuff.

Imagine going about your day not knowing what to

expect from anyone at any moment. Could be a little nerve-racking. Or it could be exciting as hell.

Try the opposite. Imagine going through every day of your life knowing what to expect from each and every interaction. Wouldn't you be bored out of your mind? I know I would.

Let's look at another side of this coin (or perhaps, another edge of this sword is more appropriate).

Just as you have everyone in your life charted out in your rolodex of personality types, you, too, are charted out in theirs.

Oh, yes.

They have expectations that you will react to certain things in certain ways, and, by golly, you seldom let them down, do you?

I don't.

A young child may always know you'll get angry if they spill their milk. Of course, your motive in setting this memory in place was likely an effort to prevent the child from spilling their milk, and to have that child learn to be more careful.

Problem is, they're really young, and gosh darn it, young ones are gonna spill their milk from time to time. So now, in their knowing ways, if they spill something, they simply try to hide the fact, cover the evidence, and hope you won't notice.

Why?

Because they know how Mommy or Daddy reacts negatively to that particular stimulus.

How about people at your work place? What do they know about you? More than know—is there anything about you so persistent that it might even be carved in stone?

People I work with know that I'm a sharp dresser with an awesome tie collection. It's true. They know that I'm always available to help out with work-related challenges.

When I was in pharmaceutical sales, my direct counterpart knew that I was really good with our sales data and that I could remember every doctor's name on our list. On the other hand, my manager knew that he couldn't count on me to remember the names of office staff members ... and that wasn't good.

My counterpart was consistently late. I made it a daily habit to forget that and still remain punctual. Someone who doesn't practice *The Art of Forgetting* might just decide to start being late, thinking, *Why should I get to our meetings on time, when I know my partner is going to be fifteen minutes late?*

How about your spouse/significant other? What can they count on about you in terms of your actions/reactions? Could they set their watch by the tight schedule you keep for afternoon tea? Do you always roll over and go to sleep right after sex? Are you grumpy for the first hour after you get home from work? Do they not function well until they've had their four-bag cup of Earl Grey tea in the morning?

You might even want to apply *The Art of Forgetting* to yourself. Forget that the first thing you do when you get home every night is to get out of your work clothes and into your PJs. Do something else. Shake it up.

Come home, get everybody in the car and go for a ride. Okay, I know in this day and age with the cost of gas and the traffic on the roads, who wants to go for a ride right after work? The point is to *do something different*! Break the pattern.

The next time your kid spills something and you want to scream, go over and kiss them instead. Okay, maybe that's not a great idea, because you don't want to reinforce a spilling habit. But, you could go over and say, "Oops. Looks like someone had a little accident. Would you mind helping me clean this up?"

I remember doing this once with my little boy and the look of shock on his face had me laughing out loud. He was so surprised that I wasn't angry with him. This was also the start to setting a clean slate for his memories of me.

How about cleaning the slate with all of your relationships?

The purpose or need for selective forgetfulness should now be apparent. But just in case it's not, here are a couple more areas where you probably already have preconceived notions that may not be of service to you.

Have you ever gone into a car dealership, fully anticipating that you were going to get taken for a ride (and not in the good sense)?

Actually, let me rephrase that. Have you ever gone into a car dealership NOT expecting to get taken for a ride? If you've ever bought more than one car, then you're probably a member of this club.

This mentality is so prevalent that there are people who make it their business to help buyers *not* get taken for that ride.

My dear friend, Matt, is one of them. He had a business called My Auto Coach and he saved people hundreds, even thousands, of dollars every day.

What's the difference between him and the average consumer? Aside from the fact that he's made it a point to be well-educated and well-informed about the auto sales process, he goes into each transaction with the expectation of winning.

Let me expound.

First, even if his experience has been that a given dealership will try to badger every last penny out of him, he knows three things for certain: 1) The goal of the dealership is to make as much profit on each sale as possible, 2) There is a bottom-line price they will accept that is often far below what most people pay, and 3) They are not going to sell a car for less than their bottom line, unless there's something in it for them on the back-end.

These three tidbits of knowledge translate into simple understanding: They've got a job to do; he's got a job to do; how can we both win?

Beyond that, it all becomes a negotiation. However, if Matt were to go into a car dealership with either the attitude of, "I'm really going to take advantage of these guys" or "I'm going to get taken in here," he'll probably be right. Either way.

Fortunately, he knows enough to approach each transaction as a clean slate.

Does he forget how each dealership interacts with him? No. Nor would that necessarily be in his best interest.

Remember, we are talking about *"Selective Forgetfulness."* It is of great value for him to remember that Dealership X always cuts right to their bottom line and saves him a great deal of time and effort. He could begin to use that dealership as his first choice each time he needs that particular make of car.

What he may choose to forget is that Dealership Y is always a pain in his ass and they seldom budge on price. Why would he want to forget that?! Because, like people, businesses change.

Perhaps not as much, or as frequently, but change is inevitable. Personnel change. Policies change. Best of all for this instance, inventories change. A car that's "hot" today, where dealers can't keep it in stock, may be so "cool" tomorrow that they can't give it away.

And speaking of cars, how about the DMV? Do you always expect long lines and poor customer service? Or for you, is it the grocery store? Or the post office? Wherever it is, I'm sure you can think of some place of business where you simply dread going. One or two bad experiences have soiled you for life—yech!

If it's not a place of business, maybe it's your in-laws for Thanksgiving or your cousins for Easter.

Whatever the situation may be, we've all got them.

Now, you may be saying, "No, that's not me. I'm a pretty positive person. I've done a lot of work on myself, and I know better."

Well, sure. If you're fully conscious 24/7 (and if the quote above fits you, then you know what I mean), then, yeah, you're already approaching each moment fresh and new. But, if you're like the rest of us, there are still some memories so deeply ingrained that they sneak up on us and catch us totally unaware.

Chapter Three

Being Ahead of Someone

I was walking down the street and bumped into an old friend who had this amazing head of _____.

Who filled in the blank and how many people simply waited for me to do it?

We are always filling in the blanks. When we do that, we are not listening.

Take the following example. This is an actual transcript of an interaction I had with a customer service rep from Dell's online support. I did correct her spelling errors, but the content is verbatim.

CSR: How may I help you?

Me: How can I find and configure a Dimension E520n online? I want a system w/o MS Vista.

CSR: Welcome to Dell Sales Chat. My name is Charina. I'll be your personal sales agent today. Give me a moment to review your concern. Please don't go away.

CSR: Hi Michael.

Me: Hi!

CSR: Actually, all our systems are pre-installed with Vista already. Including the E520. Except the XPS 710 desktop.

Me: That's not 100% accurate. I'm looking for the E520n—I was directed to it last week and now want to place an order for it. Please note the "n" after E520.

CSR: Where did you see that system? We do not carry any system with E520n model.

Me: I was directed to it from live chat (right here). I actually ordered the system and now want to reconfigure and order another.

CSR: Check on this link just to show you the systems that we carry here. http://www.dell.com/content/products/compare.aspx/desktops

Me: I see what you are saying; however, unless you have just discontinued it in the last week, I know you have an OS free system—I have one on order. Are you no longer carrying it? Can you check with someone else who may know more?

CSR: We no longer carry the Vista, Michael. All our systems, either notebooks or desktops, are pre-installed with Vista already. May I ask, why don't you want the Vista?

Me: The item number on my order is 222-5130. Please refer me to someone who knows more. My investment software does not support Vista.

CSR: Where did you purchase the system? Is it under refurbished?

Me: From DELL. No, it is not. I customized it myself. The order # is 593157137. I'm beginning to feel like I'm wasting my time here. Please refer me to someone who knows more than you do about it. Is there a log of prior "live chat" records? Perhaps you could find the customer rep who referred it to me in the first place.

CSR: Now I am getting your point.

Me: Thank you.

CSR: That system you're referring into is the N series. Am I correct?

Me: Yes.

CSR: If I'm not mistaken, this one does not come with an operating system, right?

Me: Exactly!

CSR: Alright. I got it.

Me: Thank you.

CSR: By the way, before we configure the system to you, can you verify to me your complete name, address, phone # and email address?

Me: What for? I'd like to configure it online myself. I'm heading out the door right now and would just like a link I can access later. My email address is joustnactor@msn.com

CSR: Since you're here now, let me help you on configuring the system instead.

Me: I've already taken up too much time right now. I need to go. Please provide me with the link.

CSR: Okay. No problem.

Me: Thank you.

Mind you, this was a typed conversation, and it took practically twenty minutes to get from the time where

I pointed out the "n" in the model number to the point where she said, "That system you're referring to is the N series. Am I correct?"

Let me also point out two important observations:

1) I don't think that this Dell employee was unintelligent. As a matter of fact, I'd even go so far as to speculate that she was probably pretty darn bright.

2) I also believe that she sincerely wanted to help me.

The issue was that she was lacking in her listening skills. And I would even go so far as to assert that she became this way from fielding so many calls of such a similar nature that she had become trapped in a habitual response pattern. She came to believe that she already knew what the customer wanted, or what they needed, and the possibility of anything outside of that realm disappeared.

So let me repeat: *We are always filling in the blanks. When we do that, we are not listening.*

Why do we do this? For one, we are a society of people who want things to be easy and predictable.

Now c'mon, as much as you may think you are too evolved for that ... You think, "Hey, I'm a rebel! I don't follow that BS. I like things new and exciting and challenging. I'm always pushing the envelope of my comfort zone!"

Well, sure you are. I like to think that I am, too, to a certain extent. I say "certain extent" because I know that, as evolved and enlightened as I like to think I am, I want a good portion of my day to be easy so that the rest of it can be chaotic.

I want to know when I go to the post office that I'm not going to have to waste an hour picking up a single package because of the neuroses of the guy in line in front of me, or because the mail clerk decides to freak out. I want *uneventful* for this particular transaction.

Same thing at the grocery store, or the gas station. Don't you?

Imagine how drained you might feel at the end of a day, if from the moment you got up, everything was an enormous and frightfully *new* challenge. Not a single event of your day was anywhere near routine.

A day or two of this might be pretty neat, and it could certainly happen to a large extent on a vacation to a foreign country. I'm sure you'd get a 24/7 experience of it if, say, your child were kidnapped or went missing. Not an experience I'd like to have.

So, we end up filling in the blanks because we all want *easy* —while in reality, this is a huge mistake! Easy would have been for this customer service rep to listen, without any presupposition, and think anew. Difficult is what we get when we look for easy.

Ever try to take a shortcut somewhere and end up wasting more time because you got lost or found out it wasn't as short as you thought? We do this all the time in relating to each other.

The question then, is, "How do we stop?" How do we keep our minds open to hear, as if for the first time, the voice and words of our friends, family, and peers?

Well, let me tell you this: It's easy! ... and it ain't easy.

How can it be both?

Habit!

Ever try to lose twenty pounds? It's easy to curb your eating for a meal ... to exercise for a strenuous hour, once. But to lose twenty pounds you're going to need consistency and determination and desire.

Same thing goes for keeping a fresh mind. Right now, you could do it easily if I said, "Go have a conversation with someone you're close to and hear them without expectation or presumption."

Heck, you might even be able to do it for a whole day. A week? Maybe.

You've got to understand here that this is a nasty habit that has been woven into the very fabric of our being. It is at play all of the time. *All of the time!*

I don't know about you, but I have a hard time watching a movie without jumping ahead in my mind and figuring out the plot long before the filmmaker intended. Because our films have become so dumbed-down, I'm right a great portion of the time; but I am thrilled when I'm way off base.

My point is, though, that we do it naturally, day in and day out, without even noticing we are doing it.

So back to the question of how do we stop. First of all, twinkle, twinkle, little star, how I wonder what you are. Up above the world so then you have to think for yourself. Too many times we stumble.

Pause.

Okay, you're probably re-reading that last little bit to figure out if you missed something, or if there was a typo.

I actually threw that in there as a written version of a two-by-four upside the head. To slow you down. To prevent you from doing exactly what it is you want to learn how not to do. Was anticipation leading you to fill in the blanks, jump ahead—already thinking you know where I'm going?

You may be right. And you may pat yourself on the back proudly if you are. However, you will have lost the lesson entirely. As a matter of fact, let's get that out of the way right now.

You already know everything I'm going to say in this book!

And I'm not just saying that. There is nothing I'm going to write that is highly profound or new to you, nor will you be surprised to hear anything I say. You'll probably even be saying to yourself, "Oh yeah. I could've told you that." So get over it. Right now.

Lesson One: No matter what you know, give it up when it is time to listen. Nobody will ever be nearly as impressed with how much you know as they will with how well you listen. Practice listening.

Not to something new. That's easy!

Listen to something you've heard a hundred times. Heck, if you've got a little child, have them recite their times tables to you. And you have to listen like you never heard it before! Listen like you don't know that 5 x 5 = 20.

Notice right now how your listening changed when you heard something you knew to be wrong. "5 x 5 isn't 20, it's 25!" you're thinking to yourself.

Or, worse yet, did you even notice that anything was wrong? Or did you automatically fill in the proper answer assuming it would be right?

Hearing something wrong got you riled. Excited. Something outside of your predictable. Try to listen from that space even when there is nothing new in what you are hearing. Even when your child says, "5 x 5 = 25."

Listen from the space of "Wow, I didn't know that!"

Practice! Practice! Practice!

When I wrote this book, I was absolutely all over the place. I mean *all over the place.*

I'm writing this paragraph while only ten pages of thought have managed to make it on paper. Of course, it won't look like that when it makes it into your hands, all nice and edited.

I'm telling you this because it leads me to another practice in *The Art of Forgetting.* Forget about things you've been told. There are literally thousands of these little "tenets," I'll call them, which we've been strapped with throughout our lives.

Blame it all on "They."

Whoever "They" are, I want to shove a red, hot poker where the sun don't shine. "They" have really messed us up, haven't they? You know who "They" are, don't you? Sure you do. You know what "They" say:

Money doesn't grow on trees.

Life is hard.

Time is money.

You can't have it all.

Love is blind.

You can't teach an old dog new tricks.

Those are some of the basic "universals" that float around out there.

Then, of course, there are the more complex ones. Like, you can't write a book without an outline. You have to have money to make money. Hell, my internal editor knows a ton of them. All great reasons for me to stop writing right now and wait until I "get it all together."

I listened to that guy for far too many years. If I'd kept on listening to him, this book wouldn't be in your hands right now.

And the same thing goes for all of the other things you've been told that you'd be better off to just forget. Forget 'em right now. Take out a pad and paper and make a list of the ones that have had the most impact on your life.

But wait!

Stop just a moment before you touch pen to paper.

While you may be thinking about the limiting thought you've heard a million times, I want you to write down the thought the way you'd like it to be—the way you would have liked to have it programmed into your mind. If your limiting thought had always been that "there's too much month at the end of my money," then write down something like this: "There's more money at the end of the month than I know what to do with."

If your limiting thought is, "You can't have it all," then write down something like, "I never settle for less than everything." The point is to find something that resonates with you.

Chapter Four

Learning to Forget

While attending a men's weekend with renowned author, David Deida, I shared a conversation with a friend over dinner. I had expressed a desire to establish a men's group in my home town and was quite excited about the prospect.

I asked him if he had such a group in his area and what his interests might be. He immediately went into a story about his two potential male friends. "One," he said, "is not into this kind of thing. The minute I start talking about anything spiritual, his eyes start to fog over. And the other ... he's the kind of guy who can go so far off the edge into it, that you can't ground him in what's actually the purpose of the exercise or discussion."

It was immediately apparent that my friend was

holding these men in a small framework of possibility. In his mind, he already knew what their response, and/or participation, might look like.

I invited him to reconsider his expectations of these men, and to remain open to a different outcome, thereby freeing them to be any of their possible permutations.

You might think this is nonsense. How could any outcome have the potential to be affected by the expectation of the observer?

Well, scientific research has shown that this is, indeed, a fact. The rigors of the testing have been the precursor of what is now commonly known as a "double-blind" study.

Especially in the pharmaceutical industry, studies are conducted in this fashion, where neither the participant nor the administrator is privy to the knowledge of the drug being administered.

Again, research has shown that merely by the fact that the administrator of a drug knowing whether or not he is prescribing the actual drug or a placebo will have a significant outcome on the patient's results.

Of course, the patient who believes that he is receiving

the bona-fide drug, versus placebo, is more likely to see expected results, than a patient who is given nothing. It is a fact: Expectations, whether internal or external, have a significant impact on the results.

Do you want to ask your boss for a raise, expecting full well that he will refuse? Of course you don't. Yet that's exactly what many of us do. We ask for something we want, fully anticipating a negative response.

Exercise:

Make a list of things that are important to remember and make a list of things that are important to forget!

Remember:

Fire will burn your fingers.

More than two drinks in an hour, and you probably shouldn't drive.

Your child is allergic to peanuts.

Peanut brittle has peanuts.

Green means go, yellow means slow down, red means stop!

Forget:

Your wife doesn't like your sense of humor.

Dessert is supposed to come after dinner.

Your biggest potential client doesn't like your product.

You always take the freeway to work.

Your assistant asks stupid questions.

Now, while these may seem, at first glance, to be very superficial or even frivolous, imagine the implications of forgetting even a few of these things.

You'll have to find a new way to drive to work. No big deal. You'd probably have to do that anyway, if the freeway were closed down.

But what happens when you do it? What changes take place in your bio-physiology?

Maybe not much, but at least your trip, which, for the most part has become automatic, is now an awakening event! It requires thought! Something you haven't employed on your drive to work in some time now. You've been on auto-pilot! One step away from sleep-driving.

Try this exercise!

And, if nothing else, maybe it can open your eyes to the fact that your auto-pilot exists. If it does, take it to the next step. See how many ways you shift into automatic-pilot mode.

Your interaction with your children?

Your relationship with your wife?

How about your job?

How often do you tell your child to clean up their room?

If it's anything like me, it's multiple times per day. How about mixing it up? You already have an expected result—how about letting go of that?

And, to make it simpler, how about making your request in an entirely different way?

First off, imagine that this is the first time that your child has ever left their room in a mess or the toys on the floor. What might your honest reaction be? Surprise? Sure. This is the *first time* this has ever happened.

Show your surprise (and imagine now what response that might generate in your child, who has only seen you get upset by this in the past). Play with their response. "I've never seen your room like this before. You normally keep things so neat and tidy. What's going on?"

Shift your entire expectation. Up until now, the expected mess has been the norm. What if the expected tidiness were the norm?

It is! But you have to make it that by forgetting the result you expect.

Now let's take your relationship. Demands of the job are going to require that you stay later than expected. You phone your spouse, knowing in every bone in your body that s/he is going to be pissed off!

You were supposed to come home early and help with dinner and the children. Do you call and say, "I know you're going to be mad, but I've got to stay late tonight"?

Of course not! The word "mad" shouldn't even cross your mind. So, first off, let go of the expectation.

Why are you working so hard, and so late? To make a better income and better life for you and your family. Hell, you're doing it for them in the first place.

When you make that call, you should have every

expectation that you'll be praised for your hard work and extra effort.

This is very important here and I cannot express it enough: You have to be honest about your expression! It doesn't matter what you say, if you believe that you will be reprimanded or negated, you will be.

However, if you believe that your spouse will see your hard work and dedication, she will not complain (or, if she does, it will only be an exemplary demonstration of her love for you—i.e., "But, honey, I want you home so badly.")

We've all heard the expression "the honeymoon is over," when the pizzazz has gone out of a relationship. For some couples it's gone in about six months, for others it may last a year or longer. And for some, it's over in the first week or two!

How does that happen?!

Research has shown that it is based on an individual's personality and NOT on the given relationship in particular.

Okay … it wasn't really research, but more of an

observation that led me to a hypothesis. I have a couple of friends (and maybe you know someone like them in your life) that always seem to have very short relationships.

Neither of them has ever dated anyone for longer than two years. When I came up with the idea for this book, I started to ask them a lot of questions and really began to observe their habits.

A couple of things began to stand out as similarities: For one, I noticed that both of my friends began to complain about their partners very early on in their relationship; and for another, it seemed that they both felt like they knew everything there was to know about their mates.

It started to dawn on me exactly how much of a recipe this was for disaster. They were absolutely setting themselves up for another failed relationship.

When I looked at things a bit deeper, I realized that my friends were like that in many aspects of their lives. They always had a tendency to finish people's sentences for them. Always acted like they knew what someone would say or how they would respond.

They actually prided themselves on "knowing" people (as in being able to "read" them).

Wow! The more I looked at it, the more I saw how much it had screwed up their lives. They seemed to have fewer friends but lots of acquaintances (of which I fell into).

I imagined that this had to do with the fact that I found I could only tolerate them in small doses myself.

On the bright side, they did love to talk about themselves, and other people, so I managed to learn a lot about their way of thinking.

I found that they had several issues in common. Probably the father of all smaller issues was this: They both had parents who preached to them as if they had all the answers.

Granted, this is my interpretation, but hear me out.

Both of my friends were prone to quoting their parents with great frequency. I'm sure you've heard the like: "My father always told me, never trust a man with two first names," or "My mother used to say, 'Wish in one hand and spit in the other, and see which one gets fullest.'"

We've all got one or two of these quotes up our sleeves, but these folks had dozens, and they used them freely.

Again, nothing wrong there, but it did lead me to see that they had few original thoughts of their own. A better way to put it might be that they lacked an open mind. Their heads were so filled with limiting beliefs that there wasn't much room for anything else.

Of course, in this situation, telling them so would do little good. They already had all the answers, and there wasn't any space for new ideas.

Well … that was my first thought.

Then I realized—that was their way of thinking seeping into mine. Isn't it scary how it can do that? Negative, or closed-minded, thinking can become this disgusting blob that oozes all around and tries to take over all thought.

So, quickly, I shook that off and told my friends my thoughts. I applied all of the tools I'd been developing and went into each conversation with a completely open mind, with no expectations whatsoever.

In both cases, I was completely surprised! One of my friends took everything I said completely to heart. They could see where they had closed down their mind and were actually excited at the prospect of opening back up again. The other friend acted as though they had already heard about my concept before and went so far as to say how it didn't really apply to them.

So, while I was surprised with both responses, I'm still waiting to see the results. Does that surprise you?

It might. Many people would assume that the person who was open to my feedback will make adjustments in their life and find more fulfilling relationships ahead of them. It would seem to make sense, wouldn't it?

However, we've gone right back to living in the world of assumptions if we follow that path. Reality might present us with exactly the opposite of what we would expect. It may be the person who denied my input that ultimately begins to understand and shift their world.

We really don't know until we see the results. But, oh what wonderful results we might see.

Imagine the renewed vitality of waking up to a loved one each morning and seeing them as if for the first time. You roll over to your beloved and ask, "Do I know you?" And you really mean it!

Because the truth of the matter is that you don't! And then you kiss them as if you've never felt their lips before, and you get up out of bed full of questions: What do you like for breakfast? What are you passionate about? What do you want to accomplish today? Who are those kids screaming down the hallway?

You'll have lots of questions and lots to learn about your "new" partner throughout the day, and then you get to go to sleep that night and forget it all over again.

Chapter Five

Self-Application

Here's where it really starts to get tricky. How much of what you believe about yourself is real, and how much of it is self-imposed expectations established over years of habitual patterns?

This is where you have to really look deep inside yourself and approach yourself with complete honesty. It may be helpful to have a friend to bounce some of your discoveries off of, or better yet, find a skilled coach trained in this area.

I highly recommend anyone trained in the Hendricks tools. Their skills at differentiating what is the real you versus a persona you've created are exceptional.

Perhaps looking at yourself "honestly" is not the

proper term. "Objectively" seems better suited, as it is imperative that you take a step outside of yourself and into the role of an impartial observer.

Why do you need to do this? Well, I'm not so sure that you do, but try this on for size.

Think back to your days in college or high school, or maybe even grade school. Take a look at some of your "ways" (and I use that term loosely). How did you do things? What was your approach to life? Were you an early riser, or a late sleeper? Did you exercise regularly, or were you a couch potato? Did you have a hobby or talent you were passionate about, or were you a jack of all trades, master of none?

What the hell does any of this have to do with *The Art of Forgetting*?!?

Well, just as other people will have a tendency to pigeonhole you, you may find that you went right along and pigeonholed yourself.

I'm sure you've heard the old adage: "If one person calls you a duck, you can probably brush it off. If two people call you a duck, you might want to check for feathers. If three people call you a duck, start quacking."

As cute as that may sound (and often accurate), there is another option …

Pluck your own feathers!

I mean, unless you want to be a duck (or whatever the hell it is you've apparently become), recognize the fact and make the necessary changes.

Where the problem lies is that we begin to complacently accept our new label, and we begin to quack.

Worse yet, it gets to the point that we forget who we were before we became a duck … and that's not something you want to forget!

Maybe I'll have to write a book titled *The Art of Remembering* and focus on that.

Nahhh.

There's still much more we need to forget.

For starters, and I'll use myself as an example, I have a tendency to overcome boredom by occupying my time with television. Now, I could say that it is mental downtime for me to rewind, and a part of me might accept that justification.

However, I know for a fact that when I am involved in something I am passionate about, television is the furthest thing from my mind (as is food, friends, work, etc.).

When I'm involved wholeheartedly in an activity or project, I actually find that I need very little time to rewind. The act itself is rejuvenative.

In 1997, I co-produced and co-starred in a television pilot called Badges. I was working fourteen-to-eighteen-hour days on this project and often had to be told to go home and sleep, or to take a break. And even when I did, I was so excited to get back to work that I slept very little and still had energy to spare.

I'm sure you've felt that way about something before, and some of you may feel that way about something you're involved in right now. The point is that many of our current habits are baseless.

We simply forgot something about ourselves, or we've accepted something as being "us" simply because we started doing it as a habit to fill a void at some time in our lives.

Since this book is called *The Art of Forgetting* and not that other title, let's approach it from there.

Here are a couple of examples: Using my own issue as mentioned above, my task at hand is to forget that I have a tendency to sit down in front of the tube when I'm bored.

Now how the hell am I supposed to forget that?! I *always* watch TV when I'm bored. Well, not always. Really … sometimes I eat. That's just as bad, if not worse!

Baby steps.

The first thing is to notice what you are doing. Don't make it wrong. Just notice, the next time you sit down to watch television (or whatever your habit is), what you are feeling. Are you indeed bored? Or is it that you *really* need to know whether your favorite character survives another episode? And if you *really* need to know that, then why?

Do you really care, or are you trying to escape from something?

For me, it was an escape from my fear of failure. Sure, I could take the time I'd spend watching *Criminal Minds* and work on my book; but, if I complete my book and it sucks, then I will have failed in front of everyone.

On the other hand, if I don't write it, my failure will be private and much less painful.

Or so we tell ourselves.

Are you trying to escape something? Don't worry about that just yet. Baby steps. Just notice what you are feeling when you are possessed to fall into your old habit.

After you get good at noticing, you will probably find that you aren't as compelled to keep it up.

Right now, I'm writing this sentence instead of watching TV. As much as the latest episode of *The Walking Dead* may be calling me, I've got a message that needs to get out.

Eventually, you'll find more and more of your time spent doing what you are passionate about and less time spent on trivialities.

That example is one of a self-created, self-imposed habit. The next example is one that is created by other people and later enforced by our own consciousness.

This one, far too often, strikes closer to home for most of us.

I grew up listening to my dad berate a couple of

my older brothers. I was relatively young, so I'm not certain how frequently, or under what circumstances, the berating occurred; however, it is something that stands out in my mind to this day.

As a side note, I believe the impact it had on me was to make me an overachiever, as I never wanted to hear my dad talk to me that way.

So, knowing we cannot rewrite the past, how does one forget these ingrained beliefs that we carry with us into adulthood?

Again, the first step is to notice they exist. This may take some time and effort. I'm reminded of a practice I used to employ as an actor working on a play.

I found it to be of great benefit in understanding my character if I were to go through the entire script and highlight every word or phrase that was said in *reference* to my character.

Then, of course, I would take them in context of who said them. So, for example, if my arch nemesis refers to me throughout the play as an "imbecile," a "buffoon," or a "dolt," but my girlfriend refers to me as "loveable," "silly," and "handsome," I might rule out "imbecile" and "handsome" as prejudiced and land somewhere in the middle of the other descriptives (think Jack Black, a loveable buffoon).

Next step would be to see what is actually said to my character's face. "You're loathsome" and "I can't believe you could be so rude" might give me an idea of my character's type, but, again, it must be taken in context.

Now take a look at your own life, both current and past (even distant past). What stands out as having an impact on you? Were you told time and again how "dependable" you were? How well you dressed? What a great lover you were? Or how you were always selfish and inconsiderate? Or lazy? Or boring?

Whatever it was, look at what stuck.

Now if it is something good and you like that it stuck, then, by all means, hang on to it. But, if it was something that was not-so-flattering about yourself, something you'd rather not be remembered for, then let's get rid of it.

I recently had a wonderful opportunity to witness and play with ingrained memories on several levels.

First off, though, I want to delve into another aspect

of memory and how it works. Let's look at it from a perspective that, for many of us, is much more tangible.

Muscle memory.

Athletes are masters of refining muscle memory to the point that precise and repetitive movement flows naturally and unfettered—so much so that actually adding "thinking" to the process can seriously throw off their game.

What makes the difference between a player shooting a free-throw early in a basketball game versus shooting the same free-throw with one second left on the clock and their team is down by one point?

They call it "pressure" or "being under the gun," but the fact remains that a shot, is a shot, is a shot. Thinking is what gets in the way of muscle memory.

Now, since most of you reading this are not world-class athletes (or even if you are, you're probably reading this to deal with "other" issues in your life), let's look at everyday things we do that we have committed to muscle memory.

Typing is a prime example. Even if you are a "hunt and peck" typist like me, your finger muscles are tuned in to certain movements that you process without even thinking about it.

Now try this: Type out a sentence only using your pinky fingers. Considerably slower, don't you think? Not just because you are limiting yourself to your pinkies, but because you now have to involve your mind.

While an athlete strives to get out of his/her own way by quieting his/her mind, anyone interested in living in the moment, unfettered by the past, should jostle the brain a little bit and keep it actively engaged, on the lookout for those nasty little memories that get in the way.

Back to my story and my wonderful opportunity to play with ingrained memories.

Through an interesting chain of events, I found myself on the opposite coast from my home, scrolling through contacts in my cell phone.

I decided to dial up a former lover of mine (and by former, I mean someone I'd dated fourteen years earlier and hadn't seen in at least six).

After reconnecting over a few drinks and catching up on the events in our lives, we decided to keep in better touch with each other. As a matter of fact, I even invited her out to spend a week with me in California. She took me up on it, and thus presented my space for growth.

You see, I had considered this woman (though really just a young girl when we were dating) to be the love of my life. All other relationships were judged in comparison to what we had together or, should I say, by how much I had loved her.

Fourteen years later, here she was in my life again. We were very different people, both on a spiritual path, yet at diverse stages of that development. I found that I could very easily slip into the comfort of "loving" her.

It was an "emotional" memory not so different from muscle memory. Was I in love with her in that moment? No, of course not. The truth was that I hardly knew her anymore.

What I felt "in love with" was the memory of what we had together. "Had" being the operative word here.

Yes, we were still very fond of each other.

Yes, there was definitely a connection.

Was it love? I don't think so.

But it sure felt like it, and I had to constantly remind myself to look at her with fresh eyes, to see the woman before me and not the young girl I'd fallen so deeply in love with years ago.

It took some practice, and I would be lying if I said it was easy. Yet, ultimately, I found that if I practiced what I preached, and made a conscious effort to forget what I thought I knew about her, I could get to know her all over again.

Did we fall in love again? Nope.

I can't speak for her, but I know that the feelings I had so long ago remained a part of my past.

Could we fall in love again? The possibility could have been there, yet, in order for it to be a lasting love, we would have to make every effort to forget about our history together.

Lasting love thrives and grows in the moment. It gets its juice from being completely present with another spirit here and now. Dreaming about the past or fantasizing about the future can certainly stimulate feelings akin to love, yet they are merely a wisp of what love is and are as fleeting and fragile as a puff of smoke.

This example contextually demonstrates a rather large-scale effect of emotional memory.

Now let's look at it in a more mundane nature. Where do emotional memories come into play in your life on a daily basis? How about eating habits?

Do you ever find yourself scarfing down a pint of Häagen-Dazs when you're feeling lonely or upset? How about calling friends late at night when you're sad?

Now, granted, these are considered somewhat staple activities; but in the next chapter we'll look at where they stem from.

Chapter Six

Your Turn

At some point in your life, someone (probably one of your parents) placated your loneliness or anger (or some other "undesirable" emotion) by offering you some ice cream. Of course, along with the ice cream you probably got a shoulder to lean on and a sympathetic ear.

After a couple of these instances, your memory cache associated the ice cream with the feeling of comfort you found. Later, you didn't even need the ear or shoulder, just the ice cream.

The memory was actually the comforting catalyst, and the ice cream became merely a means to stimulate or enhance the memory.

Ever notice how a particular smell can bring a flood

of emotional memory rushing through your system? Our senses, particularly taste, smell, and hearing, are very strong transducers for eliciting emotional memories.

Try it out.

The next time you find yourself bummed out about something and are ready to do that thing you do (eat a whole box of chocolates, sit through a ten-hour movie marathon, or get in your car and drive for hours going nowhere in particular), envision yourself already having the quality of feeling that these things provide for you.

It might help to get at where your habit started, but it is not completely necessary. What do the chocolates do for you? Do they remind you of something or someone special, or do they simply taste so good that you forget your woes?

Whatever it is, just imagine that you're eating them and getting the feeling that you desire. It's certainly a lot cheaper and has far fewer calories.

Now let me digress for a moment here.

The intention is *not*, I repeat, *not* to avoid your emotions.

You've probably already become quite good at that,

especially if one of these aforementioned habits is familiar to you. The point is to break the habitual process being held in place by a memory.

Eliminating the relieving activity with an imagination exercise is the first step. It requires thought and turns off the auto-pilot driving your actions. The second part becomes much easier once you've engaged conscious thought.

What is the second part?

Deal with the underlying emotional cause. Why are you upset in the first place? Why are you lonely? Why are you angry?

There are several schools of thought on dealing with these emotions, and I'm not going to favor any one over another. You may already have a very healthy way of dealing with them now and don't need another idea thrown at you.

Perhaps you're very good at dealing with anger but have a real problem handling sadness or fear. Or maybe you're great at dealing with sadness most of the time, but now and then it really gets out of control for you. I'm suggesting you try the following exercise in such instances.

If at all possible, take a very objective look at the situation, and try to find the root. For instance, I was feeling very sad a few days ago and found myself eating junk food late at night.

When I looked more closely at my sadness, I found that it stemmed from being alone a few nights in a row (my wife, Meghan, was away on a business trip).

I thought, *What's up with you? You usually like your alone time.*

A very true statement, so I had to trace a little deeper to see what was going on. The more I thought about it, the more I realized that my sadness of being alone stemmed from a college memory of having to spend Thanksgiving vacation one year on campus by myself when I wasn't able to fly home.

I spent most of the long weekend on campus reading books and watching TV.

Cut to the present, and I realized I had just started a new book the day before, triggering the emotional memory to come sneaking in unannounced and stirring up old feelings.

Once I was aware of the root of this sadness, it was

easy to let it go. Now, was I 100 percent certain that that was the cause of my sadness? Of course not.

Can we ever be certain of anything that has to do with our emotions? To say yes would be highly arguable.

I saw a bumper sticker on a car the other day that said, "Don't believe everything you think." Such great wisdom in those five little words. These words relate to *The Art of Forgetting* in many ways.

As human beings, we often become so attached to our own thoughts. We get something in our mind, and sometimes it might as well have been written in stone. We become like a dog with a bone—unwilling to let go of that thought no matter what.

Do you have any thoughts like this in your mind today? Are there any ideas or concepts that you think about that actually may not be universally true?

Or, to make it simpler, just pick one that you'd be willing to entertain as not being true. How would it feel if you didn't believe that for a fact anymore?

I just picked one for myself.

Chapter Seven

The Art of Forgetting

Take a clear, plastic container of sand. Use something that can be sealed and filled to the brim (no room for the sand to move around inside). Next, find a wooden box that is large enough to hold the sand in the container.

Now imagine this sand is someone you know. Not just someone you know, but someone you know well. Pick up a handful of the sand and hold it. Paying close attention to every grain that you can, gently pour the sand from your hand to the box again and watch how it hits and spreads. Now do this again. Were you able to *exactly* replicate what you did with the prior pour? Did the sand leave your hand at the exact same speed? Did it hit the box and spread out in the exact same way? Did some of the sand stick to different parts of your hand?

I don't think I'd be going out on a limb to state without scientific proof that it is impossible for you to recreate, with any level of certainty, the exact same experience/outcome.

People, you and those with whom you relate, are not unlike this sand. You are ever-changing, ever-evolving, moving, shifting, and flowing with the circumstances of life as it surrounds you, pours you out into experience.

Yet when we relate to other people in our lives, far too often we try to hold them into our known experience of them. It is more comfortable that way. At least it is for us, maybe not them.

What we want is this:

Pour the sand from the box back into the container. Shake the container so that the sand settles, and add more, if needed, so that the sand is so tightly packed it cannot shift. Then seal the lid.

We want to confine our experience of others as tightly as the sand is in the container. We want—even demand—to hold them to a certain limited boundary.

But don't get me wrong—that's not really a huge problem.

Why not?

Because, to a very large degree, others want to be confined to a certain limited boundary! Not everyone, mind you, but the vast majority of folks do.

It's called identity.

They may have placed their own boundaries of who they are and how they "pour out" as an experience of themselves. They may like being known as dependable or wise or exciting or, as in my case, a "joker."

Indeed, I had created a group of friends that saw me as that and still hold onto it so tightly that I find it hard not to be a joker in their presence. It is harder for me to tap into my serious and more sensitive side when I am with them.

When you notice this happening (you living into other's expectations of you), it's a really good thing! Well, the good part is that you've noticed it.

If you don't notice it, you can't correct it. And to correct it, you can either: a) talk to them about it and ask them to participate in your efforts to shift it, b) do everything you can to quietly shift it on your own, or c) turn them on to *The Art of Forgetting* and open their world to experiencing, not just you, but everyone, on an open field.

Chapter Eight

Where's Your Baby Elephant?

Have you ever been to a circus? More specifically, have you ever seen where they keep the elephants when they're not performing?

They typically drive a huge metal stake into the ground, and then connect a length of chain between the stake and the elephant's collar. History and common sense can both attest that that stake and chain are not really capable of holding that elephant down if it wants to get away.

So why does the elephant not yank it out of the ground and take off for a walk? Why does the elephant complacently remain in its place?

It does so because it has an amazing memory. Elephants are even very well known for their memory. I'm sure you've heard the phrase, "An elephant never forgets." As a matter of fact, in rank of intelligence, humans are followed by apes, elephants, and dolphins.

The elephant's brain is denser than that of a human. The temporal lobes, associated with memory, are more developed with more folds than in humans. Thus, they have an excellent memory.

We've covered the importance of memory in human evolution, but why is it so important for elephants to have such a highly developed ability to recall?

Their memory is essential even in ways that ours is not.

For instance, elephants can recognize over 200 different individuals. This is extremely important, as females depend on one another for raising their young.

When two elephants approach one another, they emit a "contact appeal": If the other recognizes the appeal, it responds and approaches. If not, it starts to agitate and adopts a defensive position.

A mother elephant can even remember who is

trustful and who is not. This capacity of recognition lasts a very long time, in some instances even long after one individual is dead. Studies have shown that even the recording of the sounds of a dead elephant attracted the attention of its relatives and descendants.

However, as with humans, the elephant's memory can also be a limiting impediment. The captive elephant, or domestic elephant if you wish, does not try to pull the stake from the ground because when he or she was just a baby, a trainer pounded that stake into the ground and chained the elephant to it.

The baby elephant tried quite consistently to free itself from this bond, but to no avail. It probably tried all day long at first, and then maybe just a few times each day.

Eventually that shifted to an occasional attempt of once a week, followed by once a month, until, eventually, the baby stopped trying altogether.

Of course, that little elephant didn't have enough power yet to handle pulling that huge stake from the ground. Over time, that memory became so cemented in its brain that it never questioned it again.

Years later, that elephant has more than quadrupled

in size and strength—but it doesn't know that about itself, and that stake and chain hold it ever-so-tightly in place.

Where in your life have limiting childhood memories been holding you in place? Were you told as a youngster that you lacked talent or that you were stupid? Were you told it enough that you've believed it ever since? What chains were placed upon you (or you placed upon yourself) when you were a child? "I just can't run fast" or "I can't sing very well."

There are also the things that society told us: "You have to work really hard to make it in this world." "You have to keep up with the Jones's." Societally, we bought into these beliefs then, just as we still buy into many of these aphorisms today.

Sadly, many of these lingering memories has become cemented into the psyche of our nation and gotten us into some of the predicament we find ourselves in today. For example, "A car in every garage, and a chicken in every pot" was the supposed campaign slogan of Herbert Hoover, as a way of pulling America out of a depression. Yet it may well have led to our excessive consumerism that threatens our very ecological system and even our planetary well-being today.

But I digress.

Let's get back to you and me, and where our limiting memories are holding us back in our relationships, in our personal growth, and perhaps even in our careers.

Chapter Nine

The House That
Memories Built

We could debate the age-old quandary: Which came first, the chicken or the egg? We could have a similar debate about thoughts and emotions— which come first?

I have dear friends that are of the mind that an emotion may arise without any preceding thought to spur it along.

Personally, I believe that without thought, nothing exists.

But it's still debatable.

The question that is more important right now deals

with your memories and the thoughts that shaped them. If you are an overweight person, which occurred first: Did you become fat and then realize, "Hey, I'm fat"? Or did you have thoughts about being fat and then your body followed suit?

I'm not postulating that we intentionally set ourselves up to become overweight. But I am suggesting there may have been some subconscious elements at play in this process.

I'll use myself as an example. I grew up in an obese family. We didn't start out that way. Really, only one of us six kids would have been considered overweight by the time we graduated from high school. However, within ten years of graduating, three out of six would be obese, and two more would be battling the up and down challenges of weight control year after year.

My father had a weight problem, mostly brought on by overdrinking, but my mother never did. Was it genetic? I don't think so. As the fifth of six kids, I was always thin and fit and very weight conscious. Yet, somehow, after I hit forty, my weight became a problem.

I can sit here and blame it on bad genes, or even just

the fact that "it's difficult to stay fit after forty." But I'm not buying either one of those stories.

I believe that I received a multitude of subliminal messaging growing up that implanted the thought, *You are fat*, into my subconscious—or at least the thought, *You will be fat one day*.

Think about it. How many times did you hear something said about you or someone you know that ultimately came to bear? I sometimes wonder if the same thing didn't happen with my hair.

I used to blow dry it every morning before school and my mom would say, "If you keep that up, you're gonna be bald someday." Now, while there is certainly proof that genetics has a great deal to do with hair loss, I can't help but wonder how much of it had to do with the subconscious (or in this case, conscious) message that I would be lose my hair one day.

Let's look at the body and mind as one entity, similar to the way a car is a combination of a chassis and frame with a motor running the whole thing. Let's consider that this mind/body is your home. How do you want to furnish it? Or, more importantly to start with, how is it furnished now?

Michael Neeley

What do I mean by furnishings?

These are the things that we hold to be true about ourselves. Let's say that my couch is my physical shape. I know that I am tall but that I slouch a bit. Perhaps that's the same as my extra-long couch, which is well worn.

There are many other things about me physically that I could say "furnish" my "house." My hair is thinning. These are facts about my furnishings.

Now, let's add on the less-than-true statements about our "furniture" that we *may* consider as "facts." My hair is thinning (fact), might lead my furniture to appear to me as "I'm unattractive" (arguable).

But as long as I hold that arguable point to be a fact, I have now furnished my house with an "I'm unattractive coffee table." Similarly, in my house you might find my "I'm really fat refrigerator."

As you can guess, I've furnished my house with lots of negative self-thoughts. There's at least two pieces of this "negative" furniture in each room.

The good news, and our first step to redecorating, is to become aware of these negative furnishings. Take a close look at the furniture that you've placed in your house. Try to recognize who placed it there.

Did you? Or did someone you know? Did a parent help you move it in, or was it some coworkers or friends that assisted you as you lugged that armoire up those steps into your bedroom?

Hey, maybe you like that piece of furniture! Maybe it's a great piece and you'll never want to let it go.

Not a problem.

Right now, we are just taking inventory.

Now take a seat on your mental recliner and ask yourself, *Is this the way I want my house to be adorned? Is this the home into which I want to invite my friends, family, and loved ones?*

If it is, great! You need read no further. But, if it isn't, it's time to make some replacements.

That's what we've been taught time and again, isn't it? If you don't like what you've got, get rid of it and get what you want!

My guess, though, is that you've already done that. Maybe even a few times. But you're reading this book, so I'll wager that you haven't found exactly the right fit for your home yet.

Allow me to propose something: You probably have already found what you wanted, but you missed one simple little problem ...

You never moved out your old furniture.

That's right. You keep adding ideas and concepts and new ways of being and excellent techniques ... and you just keep cluttering up your house without getting rid of the old furniture.

Chapter Ten

Starting Over

J ust like clearing a chalkboard before starting to write new material, it is so important to clear your slate before taking on new learnings.

In computer talk, there is RAM, which stands for Random Access Memory. The longer you keep your computer powered up and running, the more cluttered your RAM becomes.

Software programs that you open will begin to take up RAM space here and there, and eventually the performance will drop off, become sluggish, and sometimes even freeze up.

We're not much different. Our minds can become so cluttered with old programs—ones that we barely remember installing (if at all), and others that stare us in the face, absorbing our attention.

In computer-land, a good ol' reboot does wonders. It clears the RAM and starts anew with only the main "start-up" programs activated. This allows for fresh programs and software to be fired up and run smoothly, optimally even.

Can you imagine how nice that would be to do with our own minds? To clean out the cobwebs and outdated junk that is simply wasting space and preventing us from being our best possible self.

Not only would this be amazing—it is achievable!

It takes practice, no doubt. But it would be time well spent, and the results would be recognizable.

Just the removal of one limiting belief could transform your life forever. Just one flipping of a switch in which your mind gets out of the way of your being, and you could turn everything around.

This has happened to me twice in my life, and I'd like to share these stories with you as we close. Perhaps they'll inspire you to what is possible, but, more importantly, I hope they will spark you to begin your search. Find the switch that needs flipping in your life.

Years ago, when I was jousting and sword fighting for a living (yeah, I really did that as my job), I had my first "moment."

I was hired and trained to become a Knight at Medieval Times Dinner & Tournament—an exciting and fun opportunity for a young actor just starting out.

Well, to go into the show as the "rookie," you were required to learn one simple fight with a broadsword. And when I say simple, I mean about two minutes of swinging a sword and then you die. I mean, c'mon, you're the new guy—you gotta start out easy.

And I remember the first couple of months of doing this fight in the show. The arena is covered in deep sand in order to be easy on the horses' hooves and for us knights to take falls and rolls without doing serious damage night after night.

The challenge, of course, is that moving about quickly in deep sand is grueling, tiresome work, and at the end of my little two-minute fight, I was utterly drenched in sweat and entirely exhausted.

I had no idea how the other knights in the show (the experienced ones) could do that fight, and then go back out and do another—and barely break a sweat. WTF!

And then ...

One day ...

That all changed.

Not slowly, but instantly. A switch was flipped.

I went out into the arena, did my fight, and didn't even sweat.

And the only thing I can chalk it up to is that I finally got out of my own way. I stopped thinking so hard and trying so hard to do the moves "right." I stopped worrying about how I looked or if it was good— or anything at all, really.

I turned the reins over to my muscle memory (that good memory that serves us well when called upon). I got into the "zone."

And I never looked back. I never broke the same kind of sweat again, and I started doing a second and third fight in the shows.

Pretty incredible, really.

But here's something that happened more recently, and is even more mind-boggling to me, as I'm still not sure what flipped the switch.

Of course, in order to tell this tale, I'm going to have to out myself a bit here by telling you that I was not the greatest husband. Not for the past couple of years.

You see, I went through a pretty hard stretch between the downfall of my tech company and the start of my mentoring and podcasting business.

When my tech startup reached the end of our financial runway, with no new investment money to be found anywhere, I had to lay myself off. And as prepared as I was for that (yeah, I saw it coming), I was not prepared for how long and slow the transition to my new business would be.

Now, granted, in the scheme of things, it was actually pretty fast; but, when you're staring at a rent bill you just don't have the money for, time becomes almost irrelevant.

And during this struggle, I turned to worry and taking every low-paying job I could get just to make ends meet. I did this while I was building my new business, which translated into many weeks working sixty hours or more.

As you can imagine, this didn't sit too well with my wife, Meghan, who wanted more time with me for connecting and romance.

Fortunately, her business had started to take off, and she helped to cover my shortcomings.

Unfortunately, this added a layer of shame to my feelings of despair, and I felt like I needed to work all that much harder to hurry up and get out of that rut.

This spiraled a bit out of control and created a wider and wider gap in our connection.

I felt it.

She felt it.

And neither of us really knew what to do about it. So we just plowed through it, enjoying our vacation days, while the rest of our time together was touch and go.

I take 100 percent responsibility for my participation in this trap. I know I created it, and somehow, I must've known in my depths that I, too, could turn it around.

And then it happened …

Much like that day in the sandy arena at Medieval Times ...

A switch was flipped.

I stopped worrying about "not enough time" or "too much to be done." I stopped worrying about money and started to focus on the important things in life—my relationship with my wife. This woman whom I loved so deeply but had somehow lost touch with.

The change was so dramatic that I was hardly recognizable, and she even had to ask, "Okay ... Who are you, and what have you done with my husband?"

I won't bore you with the details but suffice it to say that our lives were changed in an instant, for the better.

And you can do this, too. It's not about the knowing, but more about the "unknowing." About the letting go.

About the forgetting.

If you can apply even a small amount of what you've gathered in this book, you will have the power to flip your own switch ... whatever that may be.

Just keep in mind that it is an art, and art takes practice. And with time, you will know exactly what to let go of, like the trees in fall letting go of the leaves that no longer serve them.

With practice, you will master *The Art of Forgetting.*

The Art of Forgetting

Learning Modules

Are you ready to dig deeper into *The Art of Forgetting*? I hoped you'd say that! I created these sections for those who are ready to get gut honest and do the work it takes to live the Selective Forgetfulness lifestyle. Get ready to take back the power in your life and live a life of unsurpassed excitement and joy. Let's do this.

The Art of Forgetting

A popular song from 1938, "Thanks for the Memory," dealt with a couple contemplating divorce and looking back over the ups and downs of their relationship through the years. Of course, lyricist Leo Robin didn't bother to go into the psychology of holding on to memories (both good and bad) and how they are of service, and often disservice, to our lives.

But before we get too deeply into the psychology of memories, let's go way, WAY back to the beginning. Your birth. It's doubtful that you can remember formulating your first memories; however, you know they're there. Just like taking that first step—you may not be able to recall it, but you sure as heck know you did it. And now you just go struttin' about all the time.

At about the same time as that first step, you also created memories about experiences in your life. Even when you couldn't mentally formulate them, you probably remembered that it was safest to walk close to something you could grab on to if needed. Many of us find that we still do that when we go up a steep flight of stairs, or cross a bridge on foot. Do we really think we're going to fall down? Well, probably not (for most of us); but our memory is so strong that we do it anyway.

Here's how it all got started ...

We didn't know much. Anything really. When we were first born. We experienced sensations, but we didn't even have words for them. No way of describing them, even if we had the power of language (which, of course, we didn't). However, the lack of language didn't alter our physical experiences.

We felt pain in our stomach. We cried. We felt tickling on our toes. We laughed. Somehow both crying and laughing helped us in our experiences.

Crying at the top of our lungs allowed us to move the energy of whatever pain we were experiencing at that moment. Plus, we got the added reinforcement that usually when we cried loud enough and long enough, someone came to our rescue. They helped to ease our pain even further and get us back on track to our comfort zone. More on that later.

Even laughing had its rewards. Outside of the general goodness of feeling while we were giggling away, endorphins were being released into our bodies, adding further to our feelings of elation. And just as with crying, we got further reinforcement from our surroundings. Adults would do more of the same to make us laugh even louder. They would even laugh with us, which made it all the more rewarding.

And we remembered these things.

Later, as we started to move about, we learned which things we could hold on to to help us stand up in our crib, and which ones were of no help at all. We learned what we could do with our grip and eventually, even better, we learned what we could do when we released it, as we tossed things about the room. For those of you who have children, I'm sure you've had both glee and remorse as you've watched your child experience this. How smoothly we transitioned from "Throw me the ball" to "Don't you dare throw that bowl of mushy peas!"

And we, as babies, remembered.

We weren't perfect at it. Sometimes it took a lot of repetition until we got it down pat. Okay ... sometimes it took a ton of repetition before we got it down pat. I was still telling my son at age eleven, "For the umpteenth time, will you please keep your food over your plate?" Maybe someday he'll remember. Or maybe not.

And then, from infant to toddler, we absorbed things like a sponge. Language, motor skills, faces and their expressions, and more. We were already brilliant in that we quickly figured out that the more we could remember things, the better we would be at getting what we want in the world. Heck, it's pretty hard to ask for your bottle if you can't remember the word for it. And there was great value in knowing the expression on your mama's face meant "no," even if we went ahead and did it anyway (that was half the fun of it).

And then there was school. Preschool, then kindergarten, then on to the "grades." We started to get rewarded for knowing things like our alphabet and our numbers. Counting was good and reading words was even better. And we could see how valuable it was to remember so much. Especially when we got into the grade school part where we had tests, and spelling bees, and report cards. Wow! The more I could remember, the better grades I would get. This memory thing sure does serve me well!

And it did.

It still does.

Except when it doesn't.

Sure, it was great to remember that if you put your hand into a flame, it's gonna get burned. It was ever so important to remember to look both ways before crossing a street so that you didn't get hit by a bus or a car. These things will likely never change. These memories serve us well, and I'm not advocating that you ever forget them.

BUT ... somewhere along the line, we crossed our wires.

What exactly do I mean by that?

Well, we made a shift. Not a dramatic one, but a very subtle one. We all know that words don't change. Okay, maybe new ones and derivations get added, like when a surfer deems a wave as "rad" instead of radical; but a cat is a cat and will always be a cat. We know that math doesn't change, even when they dub it as the "new" math, one plus one still equals two. Language and math—great things to remember.

And you might want to add general common sense principles to the list of things you never want to forget.

Why? Because these are the things that do NOT change. Ever! Like gravity. It's not just a good idea—it's the LAW. You don't want to forget about that law and step off of a tall building expecting something other than falling fast to the ground.

The shift I'm referring to was in that we got SO GOOD at remembering things, and that we saw the value so immensely, that transference occurred. We started to apply our memory process to things that DO change.

Let me say that one more time. We started to apply our memory process to things that actually change.

First, let me give you an example that applied to us as children. Try to recall an instance in your life where you did something wrong. I'm asking you to go with the "negative" side of the experience since it seems to set into memory much faster than the positive side. So let's say that you ask your older sibling if you can play with one of their toys. They scream "no" at you and tell you to get out of their room. Two days later, or a week later, you ask again, perhaps even about another toy. The same thing happens. If this happens a third time, you will likely have solidified a neuro-pattern that informs you that your sibling is a jerk, or that they hate you, or whatever conclusion you draw in your mind based upon your relationship and your own personality type.

Now, frankly, there's nothing really wrong with this, except ... well ... everything! Yes, you could absolutely argue that your sibling is a "whatever," and you'd have a ton of proof to back it up. BUT that still wouldn't make it true.

Argue with me all you want, but then consider this: What are the odds of a coin coming up heads when I flip it? Statistically speaking, there is a 50 percent chance of that occurrence. NOW let's say you watch me flip that coin over and over again and for twenty times in a row, it comes up heads. No, this is not a double-headed coin, nor a magic trick. It has simply, seemingly against the odds, come up heads twenty times in a row.

What are the chances that it will come up heads on the next flip? Statistically speaking, it STILL has a 50 percent chance of coming up heads.

Now a risky gambler (not a smart one), might bet you three to one that it's going to come up tails next; however, a smart gambler would know that it's still one to one odds, a 50/50 bet. Others might even go so far as to think that since it has come up heads so much that it is going to come up heads again. Our minds can play some crazy games with our heads, but the facts don't lie.

YET ... that is exactly what you have done with your sibling. You've asked them a yes or no question ("Can I play with your toy?"), and it could go either way; but, since it started out with three "nos" in a row, you've solidified that in your mindset. Your memory. But don't fret yet. It gets worse ...

Have you ever heard of a double blind study? In the simplest of terms, it is a study of treatment in which neither the patient nor the physician/clinician knows whether the patient is receiving the actual drug or a placebo. These were put into use in the pharmaceutical industry when it was discovered that the physician's knowledge of whether or not he/she was administering a placebo had a noticeably significant effect on the patient's outcome.

You've probably heard of the placebo effect, which can indeed be very strong. As a matter of fact, it was often joked in the pharmaceutical industry that placebo was the best drug out there.

Why is that? Well, quite simply, if a patient "thought"

a pill was going to make him/her better, if often DID make him/her better. Many times, it was more effective than the actual drug itself! You'd be amazed at how many drugs fail their trials because they couldn't outperform the placebo enough to be significant. But, the bigger question to ponder here is this: Why would it make any difference if the doctor knew which pill I was taking, when I'm the one taking the drug?

Once again, we rely on statistics. Time and again, it was proven that the doctor's knowledge had a significant influence on the outcome. In other words, if the doctor "knew" that you were given a placebo, s/he would somehow give off very subtle, mostly unintentional, clues that you weren't "really" getting any help. Subconsciously, they knew that you weren't going to get any better from this "pill," and subconsciously, you picked up on that and you DIDN'T get any better.

Okay, enough about that. Let me get back to you. You probably weren't even aware of it when you asked your sibling for the third time if you could play with their toy, but you had a subconscious belief that they were going to scream and say no. And fight it if you must, but at some point you will need to take ownership of some part of that response.

Now, mind you, it is a very subtle zone in which we are treading at this moment. Things not even noticed on a conscious level, but so deeply imbedded in our subconscious that we have zero clue that they are even in effect.

If you still don't believe me, it won't take long for you to do a quick Google search on non-verbal communication. You'll also find a slew of new words including "haptics," "proxemics," and "paralinguistics." These are part of a larger cadre of ways we communicate before, during, and after we are actually speaking. And I'm willing to bet that these don't even begin to take into consideration the ways we communicate subconsciously.

So the bottom line is this: Yes, you (via your thoughts) played a role in your sibling's decision. We do it all the time. Especially, if not solely, in situations where we have formed a memory that is related to what we are up to now.

Let's cut to today. You go into your boss's office and ask for a raise. They commence with demeaning your performance and tell you no way in hell are you getting a raise. Six months later, you do it again to practically identical results. By the third time you go in there, you are already prepared for a negative response. Heck, you've probably even played it over and over again in your mind, just to prepare yourself for the letdown.

Here's the thing: we've now cemented a memory, onto which we have drawn a conclusion, that this person is _____, and that is as sure as the law of gravity. Think, right now, of all of the people in your life that you have done this to. Your father? Your mother? Your partner? Your children? What are the things you say about them? My brother is a workaholic with no time for his children. My children are lazy. My spouse is a terrible driver. Of course, I'm keeping it simple here. Surface level stuff. But please take the time to think about this one and go much deeper. Don't be afraid to express what you really think. My wife is FAT! My dad is a bastard! Whatever it is, just out it. Not to them. This is about you and your way of thinking right now.

What's the point?

This: I want you to realize that you, in your way of speaking, both verbalized and held in your mind, are creating a framework (or bookends, as I like to think of them) in which this person is allowed to show up in your world. And as long as you hold them in that regard, it will be difficult for them to show up in any other way.

If you shift your way of thinking about them, will they change? Who knows? No one can say for certain. But I can tell you this—they'll have a much better chance of it. Don't believe me? Let's reverse the role now.

Back to you. What do you KNOW that people say and think about you? Let's start with your family. In my case, I was always a bit of an overachiever. I was the second youngest of six kids and the only one to complete college until just recently. Heck, I even went on to grad school just to seal the deal. I was also the only one to really leave the nest in any substantial way. I live thousands of miles away from the rest of my family, so when I go home, I have a bit of reputation to live up to. I have to come across as having my act really together. I have to know more than the rest of them. I have to be more successful than the rest of them.

Of course, this is all a load of bullshit. I don't "have" to do anything. BUT the feeling that something is expected of me is almost palpable.

What is it for you? Do you notice that you act

differently when around your family than you do when you are around your friends?

And speaking of friends … what are their expectations of you? I was always the funny guy, good for a quick joke, and constantly ready with a pun. If I didn't show up that way, my friends would probably have thought that something was wrong with me. "Michael, are you okay? Did you get bad news from your doctor today?"

What about you? How are you known amongst your friends?

Now that we know these things, we've brought our awareness of them to the forefront, we can decide if we want to change them. Do I "want" to be known as a joker to my friends? Not really. Not that I want them to think of me as a super serious guy, either. I would just like them to notice that I have a contemplative mind in addition to a great sense of humor. How's that?

Or better yet … no, BEST YET—how about I just show up as I am in that moment, and they can embrace getting to know me anew each time we hang out?

That's what *The Art of Forgetting* is all about. It's an opportunity for you, and your community of friends and associates, to show up in this world full of possibility.

It's a chance to break out of the self-inflicted mold we've created and live each day fresh and vibrantly alive. It may be a bit scary, but most worthwhile adventures have an element of that to them, don't they?

So buckle up and get ready for the ride of your life. No seatbelts. No safety net. No crash helmet. And if anybody asks if you're worried, just say "Fuggedaboutit!" (Brooklyn accent imperative).

MODULE 1 EXERCISES

What beliefs do you hold to be true about people in your life? Be specific.

Person#1 _____

They are _____

They are _____

They are _____

They are _____

Person #2 _____

They are _____

They are _____

They are _____

They are _____

Person #3 _____

They are _____

They are _____

They are _____

They are _____

Do this for as many people as you need. Consider your family, your friends, your work associates, your customers, your boss, your employees … everyone that is integral in the quality of your life.

What beliefs do you hold to be true about yourself? Be specific.

I am _____

I always _____

I am always _____

I am not _____

I never _____

Be brutally honest with yourself! By that, I mean even dig deep into what you may be subconsciously saying about yourself. Some examples: I am an overeater. I always drink too much. I am not loveable. I never make enough money. I am always late. I am not worthy.

In Module 2, we'll go deeper into what other people say or think about us; but for right now, take a long hard look and fill out these lists.

The Art of Forgetting

Since you're here now, on to Module 2, I'll assume that you did all of the exercises from Module 1. How did that go? Were you surprised at some of the things that came up?

I'm also going to jump out on a limb here and assume that some time has passed between your completion of the Module 1 exercises and right now. Ideally, you will have sat with those thoughts for about a week or so. Now, I want you to go back over the lists you created. Look them over. Feel into them. Read them aloud.

Now throw them away.

That's right. Wad up that piece of paper and toss it in the trash (or hit the delete button if you're the paperless sort). That list was "so 90 minutes ago," as my young son would say. We're moving on.

Sorta ...

Do the lists again. From scratch. Stop reading, right now, and remake the lists. Here they are again, in case you want to cut and paste them into another program or print them out.

What beliefs do you hold to be true about people in your life? Be specific.

Person #1 _____
They are _____
They are _____
They are _____
They are _____

Person #2 _____
They are _____
They are _____
They are _____
They are _____

Person #3 _____
They are _____
They are _____
They are _____
They are _____

Person #4 _____

They are _____

They are _____

They are _____

They are _____

Do this for as many people as you need. Consider your family, your friends, your work associates, your customers, your boss, your employees ... everyone that is integral in the quality of your life.

What beliefs do you hold to be true about yourself? Be specific.

I am _____

I always _____

I am always _____

I am not _____

I never _____

Be brutally honest with yourself! By that, I mean even dig deep into what you may be subconsciously saying about yourself. Some examples: I am an overeater. I always drink too much. I am not loveable. I never make enough money. I am always late. I am not worthy.

Trust me, this is not an exercise in futility. There is a point to it. If you're still reading this and you haven't done the lists yet, STOP and do it now.

All done? Okay. Review your new lists as you did before. Look them over. Feel into them with a fresh perspective, and then read them aloud.

Is the list different than it was before? Did certain pieces feel more or less true than they did the first time you wrote them? There is no right or wrong here. Your list may be identical or it may have changed dramatically. It may ring as true as the first time you wrote it, or it may feel false now. That's not the point.

The point is that I wanted you to really get into what is TRUE for you at this moment. We are changing creatures; ever evolving and shifting even in our own realities. You may have even heard that the human replaces itself every seven years. Well, while this is certainly not true, aspects of it are. For instance, your skin cells only live about two or three weeks, while your colon cells are replaced about every four days. The truth is that your brain cells will typically last you a lifetime. Good thing, huh?

But, and this is a big BUT, the wiring and circuitry of those brain cells change. Most of the time, we are a passive audience while these changes occur. They are stimulated by our surroundings and our experience. So, since things may have changed for you since you first wrote your lists, I wanted you to review them and create them anew. This is a key aspect of *The Art of Forgetting*, and one that we'll delve deeply into as we progress through these modules.

So. Now you've got your new list in front of you. You are starting to build your own awareness of the thoughts you have about people in your world and even about yourself. You've, hopefully, also gotten some grasp of how your thoughts influence the world around you.

In athletics, our eyes guide our bodies and our actions. In cycling, if you see an obstacle in the road, let's say a large rock, in order to avoid it, you look "where you want your tires to go," not at the rock. Time and again, when I was learning to mountain bike, I would end up in trouble because I had a really hard time taking my eyes off of the obstacle (usually a tree root or a deep rut). And then, BAM! I would run right into it and end up wiping out.

Another example, and perhaps you've seen this one in action yourself, would be someone like my grandpa. He was such a character as he got into his seventies, and he would love to drive us around town and tell us about the way the city had changed from when he was a kid. Inevitably, he would have the whole car load of us screaming at him to watch out, because every time he pointed to something the car would drift in that direction. He was all over the road, right then left. Scary (and a bit funny) at the same time.

Well, just as our eyes direct our bodies and our actions, our mind (read: our thoughts) directs our lives. I'm pretty sure that this is nothing new to you. We are defined by our thoughts, or in its simplest form: Whether you think you can, or you think you can't— you're right." –*Henry Ford.*

There is much more, of course, that goes into the psyche surrounding this truth. And we'll get to it through the course of these modules. However, right now I'm going to throw in an extra chunk to this equation: "Whether someone else thinks you can, or thinks you can't—they are right." – *Michael Neeley.*

Okay. Don't actually quote me on that one ... at

least, not until you get the second piece of it. You must be sitting in your chair cursing me out for a liar, an idiot, or a charlatan of some sort. You know that my statement is not true in any sort of way. And you're right. In and of itself, it is false. Until you add this: "If you believe them."

What happens when you believe what someone else says about you? Or, for that matter, when someone else says anything? When you believe it, you have given it power. When you believe someone, you have given them power. And the power of belief is ENORMOUS!

Wanna see just how enormous it is?

Try this on. Have you ever seen an elephant at a circus, or on a trip to India? If you have, you may have noticed that the elephant, a massive five-ton animal, is often kept chained to an iron rod hammered into the ground. The truth is, and I don't mean to frighten you if you are ever around an elephant, they could rip that rod out of the ground like pulling a hot knife from butter. But why don't they?

They stay put because ever since they were just baby elephants at a few hundred pounds they were chained up in this way. At first they would struggle practically day and night trying to free themselves of their chain. After a couple of weeks of that they would try every couple of days or so. Eventually, they would try once a week, then once a month, until finally they realized the futility and gave up all together. They now had the firm belief that they would NEVER be able to get away from that chain.

And now, so many years and several thousand pounds later, they don't even try. I'll say it again, the power of belief is ENORMOUS!

I'm betting that some of the things you've been saying about yourself have been around for a long, long time; perhaps even since you were a child. You created a story about the world and yourself, and you've reinforced it over the years until it became a hardened FACT.

Well, I'm here to tell you that it's a lie. It has no more truth to it than the "fact" that the elephant can't pull the rod from the ground.

But, before we dissemble those "facts" you hold true about yourself, let's spend the rest of Module 2 on looking at where we have given our power to others. It's one thing to notice what other people say about us, or believe about us, but it's quite another to accept their belief. And this is a slippery one because we may express on the surface that we deny their beliefs, but deep down we feel the truth of it and it gets reinforcement.

As if that weren't complicated enough, I'm going to throw in yet another aspect to consider. What do you "think" other people hold to be true about you? In other words, whether or not you know it for a fact (that is, you've never asked them to find out for sure) you believe that someone thinks _____ about you.

I saw this very troubling behavior one day in my niece. She was walking through a group of tables to join us at ours, and some people at another table were laughing. In her mind, she made up the story (and fully believed it) that they were laughing AT HER. This completely affected her mood and brought up both insecurities and resentment in her. Personally, I didn't believe it for an instant. The people at that table had been joking and laughing both before and after she walked by.

My niece, not having had any training to help deal with the workings of her own mind, allowed herself to go down a path that ruined the greater part of her evening. Why? She gave away all of her power. She gave it to a bunch of strangers that she neither cared for nor would likely ever see again.

And finally, let's look at the world in general. Your first thought might be, "What's that got to do with me?" Well, the truth is that the world has nothing to do with you, but you've got a LOT to do with the world. You create it! You really do, to a very large degree, generate your own reality. What you focus on in the world, where you place your attention, is what flourishes in your world.

There's a great story about a farmer working alongside the road when a man comes along heading east and asks the farmer, "What kind of people should I expect to meet in the next town up the road? I'm thinking of stopping there for a week or so along my journey."

"What kind of people did you meet in the last town you were in?" asked the farmer.

"Oh, they were a loathsome lot indeed. Never have I met such a group of liars and cheats," replied the man.

"Well ..." and the farmer paused. "I imagine you'll find no different in the next town."

And along went the traveler.

Not another hour passed before another man came traveling east along that same road. Similarly, he asked of the farmer, "The next town up the road, I'm probably going to spend a few weeks there before moving along. I'm wondering, what type of people populate such a place?"

The farmer took of his hat and wiped his brow before asking, "What sort of folks did you meet in the last town you stayed?"

"Oh," said the traveler, "they were terrific! The kindest folk you'd ever want to know."

"Well," said the farmer as he put his hat back on, "I suspect you'll find the same in the next town."

On a subconscious level, we seek out experiences, people, even a world that validates our belief system. Have you ever noticed that people who have problems (not us, of course) seem to repeat the SAME problems over and over again? Do you know someone who ALWAYS seems to get stuck in the same type of relationship with the same type of loser? If you do, you also know that all they do is sit and complain about how they can never seem to find the right one. It happens because they are caught in the trap of their own belief system. Their belief about the world around them.

There's a lot more about this to come, specifically the "Why" behind our patterns, but we'll save that for another module. For now, follow the exercises you'll find at the end of each module. These will give you the tools needed for you to take back the power in your life and to live a life of unsurpassed excitement and joy.

So let's get on with it. Here are your next exercises:

MODULE 2 EXERCISES

What do you "know" that the people in your life hold to be true about you? Be specific.

Notice that I used the word "know" in the instructions. This may be something that your friends have said about you to your face, or you know secondhand that they have said it *about* you. "Michael, I have never once seen you show up on time to anything!" "Michael, I should have known you would be late. John said you are never on time."

My best friend _____
Thinks that I am _____
Believes that I don't _____
Thinks of me as _____

My parent(s) _____
Think that I am _____
Believe that I don't _____
Think of me as _____

My boss _____
Thinks that I am _____
Believes that I don't _____
Thinks of me as _____

My partner _____
Thinks that I am _____
Believes that I don't _____
Thinks of me as _____

My child(ren) _____
Think that I am _____
Believe that I don't _____
Think of me as _____

Again, do this for as many people as you want. Consider your family, your friends, your work associates, your customers, your boss, your employees ... everyone that is integral in the quality of your life.

When you are done, I want you to go back over the list you created and mark a Y by each statement that you believe to be true about yourself. In other words, if your friend thinks that you are a procrastinator, and you ALSO think that you are a procrastinator, mark it with a Y. If you don't believe it to be a true representation of who you are, then mark it with an N.

Then, review the list once more and decide whether or not you want to KEEP that belief in place or if you want to FORGET it. So if your friend thinks that you are a procrastinator, and you agree that you are a procrastinator, you must decide whether or not you want to change that about yourself and the way your friend thinks of you. You may find that being a procrastinator SERVES you, and that you work best under the pressure of last-minute deadlines, or whatever. So keep it. However, if you find that it gets you into trouble time and again, and you lose face amongst your friends and co-workers, maybe you'll want to FORGET that trait (in this case, forget is synonymous with erase).

What beliefs do you "think" others hold to be true about you? Be specific.

In this case, you are entirely speculating. The challenge here is to only select things that you BELIEVE that they think about you. They do NOT have to be true, but they DO require that you really believe them to be true. So, if you only suspect that maybe they think you are a lazy bum, don't write it down. But if you actually BELIEVE that they think you are a lazy bum (though they would never say it to your face, right?), then write it down.

Remember, it is our belief that holds the power.

My best friend _____
Thinks that I am _____

Believes that I don't _____
Thinks of me as _____

My parent(s) _____
Think that I am _____
Believe that I don't _____
Think of me as _____

My boss _____
Thinks that I am _____
Believes that I don't _____
Thinks of me as _____

My partner _____
Thinks that I am _____
Believes that I don't _____
Thinks of me as _____

My child(ren) _____
Think that I am _____
Believe that I don't _____
Think of me as _____

Again, do this for as many people as you care to. This one will be a bit more of a challenge, and you may not be able to come up with anything. You may have such wonderful communications amongst all of your tribe that you already know, without a doubt, what everyone thinks of you. And if you don't know, at least you don't have any suspicions. That's fine.

Once you are done with this list, review it as you did the first one. If there are things that came up that a) you don't think are really true about who you are, or b) true as they may be, you still want to change them, then I suggest you embark on the first part of this journey—go to the source for confirmation. "John, do you think of me as someone that is always late?" "Susie, would you consider me to be unreliable?"

Not unlike my niece, you may be surprised that the stories you have fabricated don't hold an inkling of truth.

And finally, let's take a look at the world in general. What beliefs do you hold to be true about the world around you? Be specific.

This section deals with aphorisms and idioms. We all grew up with them. Sayings like: "Money doesn't grow on trees." "Life's a bitch and then you die." "There is no great reward without great risk." And my favorite, "If you don't control your mind, someone else will."

Go ahead and list all of the ones that you can think of that you grew up with that still hold a lot of truth for you. For the longest time, in my own life, I was held back by my belief that "you have to *have* money to *make* money." It was only after forgetting this belief that I started to break out of my financial rut.

What are the beliefs you have about the world that either serve or hinder you in your pursuit of happiness?

_____

_____

_____

_____

_____

_____

In Module 3, we'll start to look at how we can unwire the tangled web of falsehoods and fallacies that we hold on to so dearly. For now, take all the time you need to completely populate these lists.

The Art of Forgetting

Alright. Here you are again. I really appreciate you hanging in there. I'm going to make a request of you, and trust that you are smart enough to see the value in it and take personal responsibility to do it without my hand-holding, step by step.

Just as you reviewed the Module 1 exercises at the beginning of Module 2, I'd like you to follow the same procedures for reviewing your lists from the Module 2 exercises. Bring your full awareness to how the lists may have changed, if at all, and how much power the things on the list still hold for you.

The whole purpose of *The Art of Forgetting* is for you to learn practical methods for loosening the hold of limiting beliefs and to set yourself on a path of renewed existence every day.

As I mentioned at the end of the last module, today we are going to look at how to unwire our heavily wired belief system(s). If you are like me, or any other video/audiophile you know, you have probably experienced at least once in your life, such a mess of entangled cords behind your stereo/TV system that you were ready to throw up your hands in defeat. And, if you're anything like me, you realized that the best way to get it fixed was to take everything apart and start all over.

Well ... we can't exactly do that with your brain's wiring, but we're gonna do what we can with what we've got. The first step in the right direction is for you to understand your wiring. Not so much the "how"—you can get that in a good science book on neuropathic development. We're going to look at the more relevant question of "why."

Why do our brains function in the way that they do when it comes to memories? Why is it that we retain negative memories more readily than positive ones? Why? Why? Why?

I'm going to tell you the simple answer and then we'll make it harder. **Because we strive for comfort.** Or another way to put it—we want to avoid pain.

Huh? Michael, are you crazy? Why on earth would

my remembering how my ex-boyfriend broke my heart help me to avoid pain?

Now you know why I've got to take the simple answer and make it harder. It's too simple to really grasp at just a glance, so let's go deeper.

Our nervous system can only handle so much. You don't have to agree with that, but if you doubt me, I challenge you to put yourself into a highly stressful situation and see how long you last. Even professional athletes know that you can't have too many high intensity training days back to back without a good break in there. Our bodies aren't made for it.

So what do we do to avoid that kind of stress? It's called routine. We love routine because it allows us to shut down our thought process for a while. Don't think you do it? Answer me this, have you ever been driving down the road only to realize that you've just lost the last five or ten minutes of your life? You've gone off into such a daydream that you can't remember passing your old school, or whatever other landmark you may normally pass. You may have even missed your turn. It scares me to admit that I've done this on multiple occasions. And it's not that I was asleep at the wheel, or even driving poorly, it's just that my mind went off on its own little tangent and left my body to do what it already knows how to do, something it does every day—drive a car. Auto-pilot, if you will.

We act on auto-pilot far more frequently than we'd ever want to admit and definitely more than we even know. I'm not just talking about driving. It's happened to me when showering and getting ready for work. It's happened to me when I'm doing the dishes or cooking. The worst part is that it even happens to me when I'm interacting with other people.

Yes. Interacting with other people. It happens to you, too, but you're not aware of it, because you feel present, fully alert, and even attentive. This is when it happens on such a subconscious level that you'll never even recognize it. In computer jargon, it's like a TSR program (Terminate and Stay Resident). These are the programs that are running in the background on your computer while you are doing all of the foreground work. We run them all the time in our own minds.

What is your TSR? Do you have an underlying story that you exposed in the last module? An "I'm not good enough" story, or an "I'm unlovable" story? For me, for the longest time, my background story was "I'm better than you" interchanging with "you're better than me." It was a super subtle piece that affected each of my interactions as I made a subconscious judgment about the person I was relating to—were they better or worse than me? It was such a freeing moment when I was able to let go of that comparing mind and see each interaction as fresh and on neutral ground. The thought of better or worse never even entered my mind, and I was free to experience people, and myself, as entirely NEW.

But before I get too far ahead of myself, let me back up to the "why" of things.

Sometimes we are very conscious of it, most of the time we are not. Conscious of what? Our inner desire for things to flow exactly as expected. Routinely, you might say. We REALLY want to know that when we go to the post office, things are going to go exactly as expected, with no surprises. We may have to stand in line for a while; we often expect that, so it's fine. What we don't expect is a line out the door and halfway around the block. Wow! That really throws a wrench in our plans! The same thing happens with traffic. Holy crap! I've barely gotten on the freeway and the traffic is backed up all the way to here—I'll never get to work on time!

We all experience these things on somewhat of a regular basis. That is, you might get hit with unexpected traffic once a month (hopefully less), a longer line at the grocery store or post office than you had allowed time for, or any number of other things that are "out of the ordinary." No problem. We can handle it. On an occasional basis, anyway.

But now I want you to imagine a day that goes like this: You wake up late because your power went out the night before and your clock reset to midnight; you jump in the shower trying to make up for lost time, but find that you have no hot water because your water heater also shut down. Finally you head down to the car to find that the headlights were left on and the battery is dead. Your jump start from AAA arrives twenty minutes later than you had hoped for and you're finally off to an important meeting (to which you are already late). You try to call to inform them of your issues, but you can't find the necessary phone number anywhere. As you get on the freeway, you notice there was just an accident up ahead and both lanes are closed. Of course, you've noticed it too late and you can't turn around to even consider an alternate route. After an hour stuck in traffic, you try to make up for lost time by pushing the speed limit excessively. Oooops! You get pulled over and now you're about ready to cry (and you NEVER cry). The officer asks for your ID and you find that in your rush, you left it at home (along with the money that you were seriously considering offering as a bribe at this point).

Okay. I imagine you've gotten my point by now. I feel stressed out just reading about those things happening in sequence. Our neuro-systems are just not set up to handle that very well. We CAN do it; and we are sometimes required to. There are people in high stress jobs where each and every moment presents an unknown element. Some people even thrive on that. But, thrive or not, most of us don't have the capability to handle that level of stress for very long periods of time. We burn out.

Thus, we have subconsciously organized our lives so that we have periods, some short, some long, of time when we can completely relax into routine. The comfort of knowing exactly what is going to happen. Heck, not only do we relish in those spaces, we even pride ourselves on them. Not only do we love predictability, but we also love to SHOW OFF how much we can predict things.

Have you ever been in a situation where you've made a side remark to a friend, "Hey, watch how my wife jumps up and down when I tell her about my raise"? Have you ever given yourself an internal high-five because you predicted someone's exact response to your remark?

We even love for our entertainment to be entirely predictable! That's why there is so much formulaic trash being produced nowadays. We don't want surprises in our entertainment. We want to know that the good guy's gonna win, the bad guy's gonna lose, the boy's gonna get the girl, and Harry Potter is going to grow old and gray very happily. My son will often tell me what's going to happen in a program we are watching just moments before it happens, and then he gives a fist pump and shouts, "Called it!" when it does.

There is comfort in that. Predictability. Subtly, secretly, perversely, we love it.

We love it and even expect it in our relationships, too. There is something about knowing how your partner will respond to certain stimuli that allows you to relax. I mean, think about the alternative. Wouldn't you become a bit neurotic if your fiancé would go berserk over something as simple as "Honey, I forgot to pick up milk on the way home"? Well, perhaps not, if that were their normal reaction—but if you've forgotten the milk many times before and NEVER heard a harsh word, it might be unsettling.

Unexpected results are what really make us uncomfortable.

Some of you may be sitting there thinking, "Well… I've gotten really GREAT unexpected results, and that wasn't uncomfortable at all." That may be true, but I would assert that if you continually got those unexpected positive results, you would begin to wonder what was going on, and then you would start to look for the hammer to drop. Remember when we talked about idioms and aphorisms? How about this one: *When things seem too good to be true, they usually are.*

Let me put on the breaks for a moment here, before I dig myself too deep into a contradiction.

What I'm telling you about, right now, though I'm shedding it in its negative light, can actually be a good thing. And frankly, it's really everything that *The Art of Forgetting* is about. With a few more details and a lot more discernment.

We all know that there are many different types of personalities in the world, and we all have our very own likes and dislikes, aversions and desires, and outright needs. Some of us need more routine than others, while some of us may need very little at all. If you thrive on newness and love to live in a world where you never know what is going to happen next, then much of this will come as a joy to you. If, however, you thrive on the known and can hardly stand for unexpected things to happen, then you will be greatly challenged by what lies ahead.

Either way, I want you to consider that you can be pleasantly surprised by what's to come. That you do have the power to alter your world and live a life that exceeds your expectations.

In Module 4, we'll start to look at how we can unwire the tangled web of falsehoods and fallacies that we hold on to so dearly. For now, take all the time you need to completely populate these lists.

The Art of Forgetting

Language. It seems so simple, yet, outside of consciousness, it is possibly the most complex aspect of humanity when you really get down to it. And I'm not even talking about the ability to communicate with one another— I'm talking about your ability to communicate with yourself! I mean, think about it ... without language, how would you know what you were thinking? For instance, what would a cloud be (in your mind) if you didn't have a name for it? As you pondered that question, your mind probably went to something along the lines of "a puffy white thing in the sky," but oh no ... that would be cheating. You don't have a word for "sky," or for any of the colors, and you certainly have no idea what "puffy" would mean. You have no language to even know what you are thinking.

So then the question becomes ... how DO you think? Or do you even think at all?

It would be hard to imagine a newborn baby not thinking. We know they feel. Heck, the first thing they do is cry, so they must be feeling something. And then for those of you who have children know, the second thing they do is cry some more. And the third thing. It seems to be a while before they crack that first inkling of a smile. But oh what a joy that moment is. I think that is the first moment you realize you've got a real human being there and not just a milk-sucking, noise-making, poop factory.

But still a long way from language, how does that tiny little baby think? She sees a mobile floating above her crib and she is fascinated by it. She giggles and grabs and grunts and screams at it, but does she even realize that it is something that we hung over the bed for her entertainment pleasure? Does she realize that it is not a part of her, like her toes that she loves to grab and explore?

And stranger still, does she even realize that the toes she grabs ARE a part of her own body? I often wonder if it is this lack of language that keeps us from remembering things in our infancy. How can one form a memory without language upon which to hang it?

That is the crux of Module 4. The inseparability of memory and language.

It is a well-known fact that language shapes our world. And since it is also a fact that WE shape our language, we must conclude that WE SHAPE OUR WORLD. Don't believe me? Let's take a closer look.

Would you agree that the sun rises in the East and sets in the West? Would you now? Really? Well, it doesn't do any such thing, as much as we might like to think it does. The sun never "rises" or "sets" anywhere. Only our language makes it so. And the only reason that we continue to use these particular words is because they were ingrained into our belief system over thousands of years. Talk about a hard habit to break.

We, and I'm collectively speaking about humanity now, believed that we were at the center of the universe, and that everything revolved around us. EVERYTHING! And even though that false way of thinking was revealed hundreds of years ago, our language has not changed to reflect the truth.

I'm sure you've heard the quote attributed to Joseph Goebbels: "If you tell a lie big enough and keep repeating it, people will eventually come to believe it." I even find it ironic that the quote itself has also been attributed to Karl Marx and Adolph Hitler, making me wonder about the truth of who really coined it in the first place. However, point being, we believed that we were the center of the universe because we heard it so much for so long. Now, couple that with a little bit of seeming evidence (I mean, it sure does look like the sun revolves around us), and it becomes an accepted truth.

And here's the kicker—our language helped (and still helps many) to keep that lie in place. Even with the facts staring us in the face, we find it hard to buy into the truth that we are just an infinitesimally small blue dot spinning along in the universe. We still cling to that archaic language because it is so hard to let go of our belief, no matter how false we know it to be.

Okay. I'm not here to badger you about the universe nor our collective language. What I want to get to the bottom of is what "false" language you use that no longer applies to the world you are creating? Let's not drift off into denial here. We all do it. We just do it so subconsciously that we aren't even aware of it. Well, maybe subconscious isn't the right word. It's more that we've been doing it by rote for so long that we just can't remember that it's a lie. We probably heard it from our parents or from our friends, and then we repeated it to ourselves over and over again until it gained acceptance as a cold hard fact. Just like the fact that the Earth is the center of the universe.

Are you ready to shake that loose? Are you ready to wake up to some really cool reality that might even be a bit hard to swallow?

I'll start with some examples of the lies I've lived with for years. Then I want you to come up with the ones that have the most impact on your life. But that's not enough to set things right. I won't just leave you there hanging. After you've come up with the lies, I want you to figure out what the truth is. I'll also give you an example of the ones I've discovered. Feel free to adopt some of mine. I'm betting that they may apply, as many of the biggest lies seem to be universal.

Have you ever said to yourself, to your partner, to your child, or to anyone else, "I can't afford it"? That was pretty common with me growing up. It could be as simple as me asking my Dad to buy me a skateboard and him saying, "We can't afford it," to my mom saying, "Let's take the kids to Disneyland," and him replying,

"We can't afford it." It was one of those lies that felt so very, very real.

I'm sure some of you are reading this and agreeing with my dad and perhaps even slightly astonished that I could call him out as such a liar. Well … too bad. But don't get me wrong. This isn't about badmouthing my dad. I'm sure it was a lie that was passed down to him from generation to generation. I still fall into that lie on occasion and only through my practice do I consistently come back to the truth.

What's the truth, you ask? The truth is that we COULD have afforded both the skateboard AND Disneyland. The lie was just more convenient than telling me that what he really meant was that it was not as much of a priority for him. That's the slipperiness of this lie and many others just like it. They are just so much more convenient than going into details; and let's face it, we're often too lazy to take the time for details.

Here's the real rub, though—my dad didn't even know he was lying! He didn't. To him, it felt like the truth because he had already budgeted money for so many other things that there was none left for the skateboard or Disneyland. Remember the center of the universe lie. This was the same clown in a different suit. A little bit of evidence made it all look real.

And now for the saddest part of this whole vicious cycle: The lie prolongs itself and makes change even more and more difficult. When you stay in the language of the lie, it becomes impossible to break away to a new possibility. In other words, so long as my dad kept using the language of the lie, he would NEVER be able to afford these other things.

So there's your first lie: "I can't afford it."

Do you ever use this one? If not, don't worry, we'll find one that you do. But for now, let's get rid of this one.

So, if it is a lie (and we are all agreed that it is a lie) then we have to figure out the language of the truth. But before I lose some of you that are really clinging onto this one, let me add that YES there are some things that you may TRULY not be able to afford (right now). There probably always will be. I cannot afford to buy a private jet (not that I would choose to if I could). Even the wealthiest among us, unless you are Bill Gates, could not afford to buy the Queen Mary II. Let's be real and stick to the simpler things that we are usually talking about when this lie possesses us.

My son will be turning sixteen in a few more years, and he's already going on about cars. He loves the Ford Mustang, and I'm sure he'll try to find a way to get me to buy one for him. Can I afford it? At first blush, you could look at my finances and say, "No way"—especially once you add on what his insurance is going to cost me. However, for me to deny him by saying that I cannot afford it would be a lie. One that I do not want to propagate.

Instead, I will tell him that I am choosing to spend my money on other things. My intention would be better to put the same amount of money toward his college education.

No kids? Try this one on: would you rather be driving a Ferrari or a Range Rover instead of the Toyota you are driving right now (insert your own makes and models)? Is your knee-jerk reaction that you can't afford to drive a $100,000+ car? If so, I would say that you are lying to yourself. There's probably not a single one of us taking this course right now that couldn't be driving a luxury car if we wanted to. We simply make wiser choices with our money in our current situation.

Trust me. I had an employee working for me back in

1992 that was driving a Maserati—and it wasn't because I was paying him a lot. It was because of his priority. He lived in a crappy little apartment that he shared with three other people. His clothes were out of style and worn, and he had very little else to his name. He only cared about how he looked driving down the street. It gave him all of the ego boost he needed. Hey, to each his own. The point is that if he could afford it, you could afford it, I could afford it. The truth is about choices, so let's stick to the truth.

So, here's your first truth: "I'm choosing to spend my money on something that is more important to me."

Want to tackle another lie? This one is a bit more personal to me, so it may not resonate with as many (if any) of you; however, I'm guessing that you might find a similar flavor of the lie. Another way to describe this particular type of lie is to call it a "story." You know, the stories we tell ourselves about the world. Our world, in particular.

My story was that *women cheat on me*. Now, I want to call your attention to the specificity of my story's particular language—women cheat "on me." I point this out so that you can recognize that I did not in any way think that ALL women were cheaters. No, sir! It was ONLY the women that I happened to get romantically involved with. OTHER women were great! Everywhere around me I saw terrific women in fabulous, trusting relationships. Hell, who do you think I was looking at when I got into the relationships anyway?!? I didn't consciously seek out women that were going to cheat. That would be crazy!

Yet, it seemed to happen over and over again.

My story about this started when I was a junior in high school. My girlfriend and I were out on a hot date. I'd saved up enough money to take her out to one of the town's finer dining establishments for her birthday. I got dressed up in the nicest threads I had for a seventeen-year-old, and even brought her flowers. Everything was going great until about halfway through the meal, she started to complain of not feeling well. This went on for about fifteen minutes before she asked me to take her home. No worries. Of course, I didn't want her to be out and about if she wasn't well. So off we went.

However, the night was still young, as was I, so I headed down to the local burger joint where you could almost always find some of the high schoolers hanging out on a Friday night. Twitter and Facebook didn't exist yet, and this was even pre-cell phones and PCs, when we hung out in a real place instead of a chat room. I ran into my best friend there and decided to sit down with him and steal some of his fries while he downed a cheeseburger.

I swear, I was not there for more than fifteen minutes when my girlfriend walked in with another guy. I couldn't believe it! Are you kidding me?!? Not only did she have the gall to lie to my face, but then she even had the audacity to show up in a well-known spot with someone else by her side! Oh, the shame! The disgrace!

Okay, I'm exaggerating a bit. Just for fun. Sure, it hurt at the time. It hurt a lot. After a short confrontation, the relationship was immediately over. Of course, the healing took quite a bit longer, but I did eventually get over it.

Cut to a few years later. I'm now a happily married guy. That is, until I caught her in bed with another guy. I won't drag this story out. Suffice it to say, that relationship also ended quite abruptly.

Then only a few years after that, I had another experience of a woman cheating on me. Only the details changed, but the outcome was always the same. It was really starting to take its toll on my self-esteem.

After the fourth time that this happened to me in relationships in which I was totally invested, I now had my story firmly in place. You heard it. Women cheat on me. End of story.

It took me a few years and a lot of books and study from the self-help section before I started to figure it all out. My first discovery being that "I" was the common denominator in all of the scenarios. That's right. The women were consistently different. Not even the same types, really. I was the only recurring character in each chapter of that story. One of those things that make you go, "Hmmmmmm???"

So, as I started to wonder about it, I also started to look at what my participation was. I realized that the first or second time was probably a complete fluke. Maybe a poor choice in partners, and probably could chalk a lot of it up to youthful folly. But having it happen three, four, five times in a row? What was up with that?!?

The deeper I delved into it, the more I realized that I was starting to manifest it in these relationships. I "believed" that I was going to be cheated on. It was very subtle and subconscious, but it was most definitely there. And it wasn't until realizing this that I was able to deal with it. Until I was able to replace a falsehood with a truth.

Of course, it was false that all women cheat on me. I'd been in plenty of relationships where that didn't happen. This provided another key learning that helped me in shaping my book: *It is the negative experiences that have a much stronger impact on our memories and the formulation of the underlying belief system.* Sadly, we tend to forget our positive experiences. Not completely, of course, but they definitely take a back seat to the negative ones.

Try this one on: Isn't it always the case that when you are getting ready to get out of a relationship, you can only recall and think about the bad times? It's even weirder that then in some ironic twist, once you are out of the relationship, you can only remember the great times. Aha! There's the catch in that nasty hook. We get lured back into repeating our mistakes by our fond memories, blotting out the bad ones momentarily. We become destined to repeat our stories ad infinitum.

Well, that is, until you pluck that hook from your

mouth, open your eyes to the real truth, and forget about the lie you've been telling yourself for so long.

Enough about my lies/stories. On with the exercise in finding your own. I've created a form for you below, filling in my lies and truths to get you started. Use this format, and take your time in finding the really juicy ones. The ones that have been clinging for so many years. With some practice, you'll even be able to uncover the deeply hidden ones. You don't even know they are there ... yet. But with time and practice, you will uncover them and unlock a life of ever-expanding possibility for yourself.

Here we go ...

LIE / OLD STORY	**TRUTH / NEW STORY**
I can't afford it.	I'm choosing to spend my money elsewhere.
Women cheat on me.	I attract and maintain loving and faithful partners.
Now your turn ...	
_____	_____
_____	_____
_____	_____
_____	_____
_____	_____

Feel free to go to town on this one. By that, I mean that you needn't go into exploring how true it is or isn't—just blurt them out there. You'll get a feel for how much hold they have on you when we go through exercises for this in another module. The truer they are for you, the harder it will be to let them go, AND possibly even recognize them. Until I saw it for myself, I would never have believed anyone that told me that I was responsible for being cheated on in my relationships. I would have argued that I had absolutely NOTHING to do with it and that I was simply the victim. Yuch! I can hardly even say that word now. I feel all slimy when I even consider myself as being a victim. Really?!? I mean, c'mon, whose life is it anyway? Was I really so weak that my external circumstances were out of my control and I was entirely at the effect of my surroundings? Wow! Talk about taking on a defeatist attitude and giving up hope.

Anyway, before I digress too much, go for those. The ones that you might even find yourself arguing to defend. If there is any point in your life and relationships (work, home, or play) where you feel that you are not understood, or that you are taken advantage of, or that you are stuck—that's where you want to look. That's the juicy one that I'm talking about.

So … get to it!

We'll start to look at removing the hook and unwiring the lie in our next Module.

The Art of Forgetting

Wow!

That was quite a list you made. Of course, I can't really see it, and I'm only speculating. So … if you didn't make "quite a list," please do it now. Seriously, folks! This is where the rubber meets the road. The number two reason that people keep buying self-improvement books is that they fail to follow the actions prescribed for success. The number one reason they keep buying self-improvement books is that even after they've followed the prescribed actions, they give it up after a week or two or a month.

I can't help you with the number two reason. I can't show up at your house or office and coerce you into following the exercises I've given. That part is entirely up to you. But I can tell you this: If you'll take responsibility for the second top reason, I can help you with the top reason. That's what *The Art of Forgetting* is about. I promise that if you follow all of the prescribed work in these modules, the things you learn on your future path of self-discovery will have a much more profound and lasting impact upon your life.

Okay. My apologies to those of you who have diligently completed your exercises without any additional prompting. However, as any good coach, I've got to keep the pressure on to get the desired results for EVERYONE.

Moving on …

So, now that you've figured out some of the lies you live with, the stories that have shaped, and even become, your reality, how do we shake them loose? That's the tricky part. What makes it so tricky is that it is really so very simple. On paper, anyway. On paper, it can be summed up in a word or two. You must become "ever aware." Awareness. That's it in the simplest form.

Like I said, though, it looks and sounds a lot easier than it really is. And here's why: not unlike the movie, *The Matrix*, we are so drawn into and comfortable in our "unreal" world that breaking free from it is just too terrifying and, well, too damn much work. It's SO easy to just stay stuck where we are. We default to thoughts like, "It ain't all that bad now, is it?" or "Things could be a hell of a lot worse."

Ahhh, the web we weave.

Awareness. If you've ever practiced meditation before, you know how fleeting it can be. One moment, you are concentrating on your breath, feeling your lungs expand and collapse, totally present with what is. Then, WHAM! Your mind is off wandering. Thinking about all of the things you need to get done. Worrying about your finances, or your health, or your kids. Perhaps you even begin writing the great script of your life as you'd like it to be, playing and replaying scenes with your partner or your boss until it goes exactly as you envision it.

Of course, this happens even when we're not meditating. It can happen when you're driving your car, doing the dishes, walking the dog, taking a shower, ANYTIME, really. It's what our mind does. In Buddhist philosophy, we actually have six faculties:

1. We see with our eyes.

2. We taste with our tongue.

3. We smell with our nose.

4. We hear with our ears.

5. We touch with our skin, AND

6. We think with our mind.

It is what the mind does.

Have you ever pondered the difference between the mind and the brain? Briefly, let's just look at the two. Your brain does all types of things that you have zero awareness of and zero control over. It regulates your hormones, keeps your body functioning, controls your reflexes, and performs many other functions that do not even require thought.

Then, there is somewhat of a middle ground. We know that if we want to move our body, let's say raise an arm, it begins with a signal in the brain. We consciously choose an action and the brain kicks in to help us perform that action by sending the right signals through our nervous system. There are a number of things that we do consciously, utilizing our brain as a tool.

And then there is thought. Where does it occur? I mean, REALLY occur? Some people would argue that they "think" with their heart, or with their gut more than their head. Probably everyone would agree that at some point or another in their life they have sensed something in their mind that was not entirely inside their body. That feeling you get when perhaps your neck hairs stand on end, or your heart leaps from your chest when you fall in love. Sure, science can explain away a great deal of these feelings, but certainly not everything. Just as the mind cannot be considered to truly only exist in the brain. The mind and brain are two very different things.

So, back to the mind, then. Its job, if you will, is to produce thought. That's what it does exceedingly and pretty much non-stop. Sometimes it goes off on auto-pilot, while at other times, we are there at the wheel steering it in the direction we want to go. Even then, it may get sidetracked from time to time, but we are definitely at the helm.

Memory is like nature's cruise control for your mind. It allows you to function with minimal effort, thus producing a more comfortable state of being in the world. It's a good thing, and sometimes a great thing! It has helped us, as a species, to survive and rise to the top of the food chain. Imagine if our caveman ancestors were to forget which berries were poisonous, or which animals were most dangerous. We would have surely died out long ago. But thanks to our excellent observation coupled with a keen memory, we are alive and kicking still today.

Our memory was our most powerful tool, and we wielded it wisely. However, at some point, that one-edged axe became a double-sided sword. It began to cut both ways, as the expression goes. Unwittingly, we started to do harm to ourselves. It was almost like we started swinging the blade about randomly. If you've ever seen young kids playing with foam swords, you know exactly what I mean. Anything and everything in sight is in grave danger of being assaulted.

What we did was, we stopped cataloging memories into their proper places. You see, most memories that serve us as tools were very finite elements. They were the things that didn't change. Things like: "fire will burn you if you get too close," "a knife will cut you if the blade drags across your skin," "jumping or falling from too high up in a tree will break your limbs or kill you." You know, the important things that kept us alive and safe.

We also had a set of memories that were NOT tools. "I remember that my first cat was yellow," or "I remember that your eyes are blue and your birthday is tomorrow."

Things like that. Little factoids. The similarity was that these things ALSO did not change.

And THEN we have a set of memories that are NOT factoids NOR words to live by, but are experiences. I call these the jumbled ones. The mixed signal ones. You can see that it would be easy to get them mixed up. I mean, some of our "experiences" are what lead us to the words to live by. Many times, especially as rebellious youth, we test the words to live by with real-world experience just to see if it really is true. Most of us only test these once, and that is enough. Others take up careers as daredevils, constantly flirting with death.

This jumbled class of memories include things about people we know. On a grand scale, here are a few that we typically take for granted: Politicians are liars. Lawyers are crooks. Corporations are evil. We call these "stereotypes." And sadly, stereotypes are most often supported by a thread of truth. Of course, we know that not all politicians are liars, not all lawyers are crooks, and not all corporations are evil. BUT the stereotypes have become so pervasive in our society that we have a deeply seated, subconscious shred of belief that they are true. We always want to confirm the things our politicians tell us. We'll often look into a corporation's background in order to be sure that we want to do business with them or support their products.

On a scale much closer to home, who in your life fits these stereotypes: So-and-so is a "jerk"; _____ is "lazy"; what's-his-name is a "know-it-all"?

And closest to home—what about yourself? What stereotypical personas do you fall into? I've been known to procrastinate. That WAS one of my personal features, if you will. But quickly, before we move on, I want to bring your attention to two little pieces here. 1) I didn't say "I procrastinate" or "I am a procrastinator"; and 2) I did say "was." These little bits of language choices are very important to distinguish. What we say about ourselves, and how we choose to say it, are extremely important.

So think about your stereotypical personas for a bit. We won't dwell on them right now. The important thing here is just to notice.

Tune into your body.

Get feedback from your community.

Follow your instincts or urges (consciously).

Use the next few pages to explore and write down

all of the things about yourself, your associates, your family, and so on. Track the things that you want to keep and those you want to let go of once and for all. Remember—do this both for yourself and for others.

If you really want them to be able to change, you'll need to let go of the way you see and believe them to be.

And for more insights about much of what I've covered in this book, be sure to tune in to my podcast, "Consciously Speaking," where *The Art of Forgetting* is a common thread through many of the discussions.

_____

_____

_____

_____

_____

_____

_____

_____

_____

_____

_____

_____

_____

Michael Neeley

CERTIFICATE
for
FREE TICKETS

Michael Neeley, founder and CEO of Your Authority Blueprint, cordially invites you and a friend to attend one of our live events as our guest. Please go to www.YourAuthorityBlueprint.com/Gift to register today.

If you do not have access to a computer, you may contact us at 831-236-6868 to register over the phone.

This offer is available to all purchasers of "The Art of Forgetting" by Michael Neeley. This offer is limited to the Your Authority Blueprint Live event only, and registration to the event is subject to availability of space and/or changes to the schedule or program. This is a limited time offer, and may or may not extend to events beyond the date shown above. The value of this free ticket for two people is $1,994 at the time of printing, and is subject t change. Participants are responsible for travel to and from the event, and for meals while on location. A refundable seat deposit will be required upon registration in order to secure your seat. This deposit will be refunded only upon your arrival at the event on the first day. This is in order to prevent "no-shows" and to be able to provide the venue with an accurate attendee count.

Ut hillupt assinvendunt incti utem facia con reraes ut es sequisseque nos doluptat.